National Heritage Inventory

AREAS OF SCIENTIFIC INTEREST IN IRELAND

An Foras Forbartha
St. Martin's House
Waterloo Road
DUBLIN 4

Sponsored by
The Heritage Trust

ISBN 0 906120 50 0
July 1981

Price: £3.00

CONTENTS

1. INTRODUCTION

One of the principal recommendations contained in The Protection of the National Heritage (An Foras Forbartha, 1969) was that the preparation and publication of a comprehensive and systematic record of the national heritage should be undertaken.

The need for such an inventory was clearly stated in the report. Ireland has a remarkable heritage of historic and scientific sites, varied in type, widely spread over the face of the country. This heritage is of growing importance for purposes of education and recreation, not only in the daily lives of Irish people, but also in the development of tourism and the pursuit of historical and scientific research. It is, however, being steadily whittled away by neglect and natural forces on the one hand, and by human exploitation, pollution, and other aspects of modern development on the other hand. This could represent a serious loss to the nation, since the heritage, properly cared for and suitably developed, could bring many and continuing benefits to present and future generations.

An Foras Forbartha undertook the responsibility of preparing the National Heritage Inventory. Since 1968 it has carried out surveys of both the natural environment and man-made structures. Detailed county reports concerning areas of scientific interest*, buildings of architectural importance and sites of archaeological interest have been completed for the local authorities, and made available to relevant Government departments and state agencies. Much of the information contained in these reports has been incorporated into the County Development Plans prepared under the Local Government (Planning and Development) Acts, 1963 and 1976. In addition to the county reports a national inventory of landscapes, Inventory of Outstanding Landscapes (An Foras Forbartha, 1977), has been published. Detailed architectural inventories of Cobh (1979), Kinsale (1980), Carlow (1980), Bray (1980) and Tullamore (1980), have also been published.

In addition to these reports a national report entitled Peatland Sites of Scientific Interest in Ireland (An Foras Forbartha, 1980), drawing upon the county reports, was prepared at the request of the Wildlife Advisory Council.

A National Heritage Inventory Working Party was established in 1969 to co-ordinate State activity and to prevent duplication or overlap in the work. Members of the Working Party were:-

---

* An area of scientific interest is a site with natural or semi-natural features of ecology, geology or land-form. It may be valuable for supporting communities or populations of characteristic or endangered plants and animals, useful in describing the processes or factors that govern their appearance or important in interpreting the structure of land and its origins.

Mr G Bagnall	Bord Failte Eireann
Dr D Cabot (Chairman)	An Foras Forbartha
Mr B Drury	Department of the Environment
Dr A Flegg	Geological Survey
Dr M Gardiner	An Foras Taluntais
Mr T Lee	Bord na Mona
The late Comdt P J Madden	Ordnance Survey
Dr C Moriarty	Department of Fisheries & Forestry
Mr O Mooney	Department of Fisheries & Forestry
S Mac Carthaigh, Uas	Office of Public Works
Ms M O'Shaughnessy	Department of Fisheries & Forestry
Dr A O'Sullivan	An Foras Taluntais

The purpose of the national report on areas of scientific interest is to make available to the public and other interested parties a summary of the information contained in the county reports. It is hoped that the information will be a valuable aid to planners and managers in reaching decisions about the future use of land. The report also acts as a baseline against which future changes in the quality or importance of sites can be measured. A set of the detailed county reports is in the library of An Foras Forbartha where it can be consulted.

This report can be viewed in relation to the two critical dates contained in section 24 of The Protection of the National Heritage (op. cit.). The first was 1970, designated European Conservation Year by the Council of Europe. It was suggested that this event should be used to launch an enlarged conservation effort in Ireland. This was done and additional effort was directed towards inventory work. Secondly, 1978 was suggested as the date for the completion of a detailed inventory "to illuminate long-term action before too much of the heritage is lost or damaged irreparably". The publication of this and other inventory reports provides the necessary information for the basis of a national conservation programme.

The photographs came from the following sources:-

Bord Failte (Plates 1,5,8,12,14,18,19,23,29,32)
Dr D Cabot (Plates 2,4,7,9,11,13,15,16,17,21,22,26,30)
The Director in Aerial Photography, Cambridge University
(Plates 3,6,10,20,24,25,27,28,31)

David Cabot
Head, Conservation and Amenity Section
Planning Division

April 1981

2. METHODOLOGY

(a) Sources of Information

Literature and field surveys of areas of scientific interest have been in progress for many years, carried out by the staff of An Foras Forbartha. Experts with detailed information have also been consulted and invited to supply information.

Members of the National Heritage Inventory Working Party contributed extensive and valuable information. Reports were received from:

Dr A Flegg (Geological Survey)	-	Geological Sites
Mr O Mooney (Forest & Wildlife Service)	-	Woodlands on State lands
Ms M O'Shaughnessy & Dr C Moriarty (Fisheries Division)	-	Freshwater ecosystems
Mr T Lee & Mr T Barry (Bord na Mona)	-	Peatlands
Dr A O'Sullivan (An Foras Taluntais)	-	Grasslands

Additional information was received from:

Mr T Barry & Dr P Fitzmaurice (Central Fisheries Board)	-	Freshwater ecosystems
Dr J Bracken (University College Dublin)	-	Project Aqua sites
Dr J Laundon (British Lichen Society)	-	Lichen sites
Dr J Westermann (Netherlands Commission for International Nature Protection)	-	Wetlands

The team in An Foras Forbartha - consultants and staff - responsible for gathering information and preparing reports was:- Professor W Watts, Ms A Quinn, Dr D Cabot, Mr R Young, Mr R Goodwillie, Dr E Fahy, Ms L Farrell and Mr T Curtis. Additional assistance with specific information was supplied by Mr D Synnott and Ms M Scannell (National Botanic Gardens), Dr D Naylor, Dr F Synge and Mr W Warren (Geological Survey), Dr J Jackson and Mr R Sheppard (An Taisce), Mr C Breen and Mr D Doogue (Dublin Naturalists Field Club), Mr D Scott, Mr L Stapleton (Irish Wildbird Conservancy), Professor D Webb, Dr G Sevastopulo and Dr D Kelly (Trinity College, Dublin), the staff of the Forest and Wildlife Service and the county recorders of the Botanical Society of the British Isles. It is impossible to acknowledge all the generous assistance at county level which was given towards preparing the county reports but it is nevertheless appreciated. This summary report was compiled by Dr A While, Dr D Cabot, Mr N Taylor and Dr C Lloyd. Mr R Goodwillie extensively revised it; content.

(b) <u>Criteria for Inclusion and the Layout of the Report</u>

The areas of interest are listed by county and classified by habitat so as to be useful both to the tourist and the specialist. Counties are arranged alphabetically, Tipperary being split into its two administrative regions, the North and South Ridings. Within each county the areas are divided into four ratings of importance, international, national, regional and local, and again listed alphabetically.

1. <u>Evaluation of areas</u>

The criteria used for the evaluation of ecological sites are now generally accepted to be the following ones which are not necessarily listed in order of importance.

(1) Naturalness

No part of our countryside today is untouched by the hand of man or his grazing animals and the concept of natural vegetation is not tenable for any sizeable area. For example, a good proportion of the Irish flora and fauna has been introduced by man (about 25 per cent of flowering plants and 35 per cent of mammals) and these organisms have integrated themselves into the pre-existing communities. Research is gradually revealing the types of community that developed before the coming of man and the degree to which an area approximates to this state is one of its most important values.

(2) Richness or diversity

This applies both to the number of species in a community and to the number of communities in an area. The most natural examples of any community have all available niches filled by the species most suited to them. They are thus species-rich relative to that community type in general. Variation in communities within the site is also relevant. Apart from it being more interesting to see several different communities in an area, provided each of them is developed properly, it is clearly better to choose one site with a range of variation rather than two or three separate but homogeneous ones.

(3) Rarity

The variability of environmental factors means that the extremes of any gradient, say of grazing or wetness, are found only occasionally. Rare combinations of factors give rise to rare habitats which may be indicated by rare species or unusually large numbers of a common one. Rarity for its own sake can be over-rated but the exceptional habitat or species may reveal a widespread truth that is otherwise difficult to see. It is an important element in coserving the full range of variation of natural communities.

(4) Typicality

The typicality of an area is at least as important as rarity for planning and conservation where lands are being reserved in the long-term for the sake of their natural communities. If most of the examples of a habitat are going to be destroyed or greatly modified, it is important to retain some of those at the centre of the variation as well as at the extremes.

(5) Size

In a changing environment subject to intensification of use, size is of the utmost importance. A large enough area will prevent outside influences from modifying the feature of value. All conservation sites should be surrounded by a buffer zone in which these influences can be absorbed without affecting the heartland. Nutrient-poor sites, such as bogs and wetlands in general, are especially sensitive to interference in this way.

(6) Scientific research

All other things being equal, the existence of scientific records adds to the value of an area. They will make subsequent work easier and more revealing and they may allow an estimate of change over time to be made. Time is an environmental factor that cannot easily be simulated by experiment.

(7) Accessibility and education

These criteria on their own are not of great importance as almost any area can be made accessible if it is so desired and used for education. However, they may be useful in choosing between otherwise similar sites.

A somewhat longer discussion of these topics may be found in Ratcliffe (1977). He also lists fragility, potential value, intrinsic appeal and proximity to another valuable site as criteria of importance.

The use of these criteria in evaluating an area for its ecological, and insofar as they apply, its geological interest must be largely a subjective process at this stage of our knowledge. All the factors are difficult to quantify and they vary in significance from one habitat to another. Nevertheless, it was found in practice that the separate members of the survey team came into close agreement as the work progressed. Early inconsistencies were removed in the preparation of this report and it may be noted by those who know the county surveys that some existing sites have been re-rated and that a few additions have also been made. These changes have arisen by reason of new information becoming available and by a process of rationalisation when all the examples of a certain habitat could be compared together.

The attempt has been made in site evaluation to arrive at an overall ecological rating for an area rather than to depend wholly on one group of organisms or another, although there are obviously exceptions to this rule when one feature outweighs all the others. It will be noticed, for example, that bird populations are sometimes described as of international importance when the area in which they occur is given a lesser value. This stems from the fact that a scale for waterfowl already exists which is based strictly on numbers. It has been conventiently summarised by Hutchinson (1979). In the extreme case such numbers can be built up by artificial feeding or by pollution, circumstances that are not linked necessarily with inherent ecological interest. The waterfowl scale has therefore, been taken as a guide to the importance of areas but not as an absolute rule. Other international guides that have been used include the Council of Europe and E.E.C. handbooks on endangered species (See Bibliography).

The internationl, national, regional and local ratings are labels for a four-point scale of importance. International sites will score highly on most of the criteria listed above. They are the best Irish examples of a certain type of community or feature, the largest concentrations of birds, or a phenonemon or structure that does not occur elsewhere. A visitor from abroad would come specially to see such a site which is irreplaceable. The scale then descends to national sites which any Irish worker on the subject would have to examine but for which a replacement area could sometimes be found. Regional sites are particularly good areas, useful in understanding the features or vegetation of a province, but which occur relatively seldom. Local sites have one or two items of interest and are better examples than the multitude of areas that are not listed at all. They often are of value in education and may have been little investigated in the past.

2.   Identification of Areas

The naming of areas often presents a problem since so few of them have names, even on the large scale maps. The principle has been to use the townland name if no better one exists. The grid reference is given for the centre of the area and it is expressed as a six figure reference if the site is smaller than 10 ha. The area in hectares is then given but if the site is a linear one, a coastal section or a length of cave passages, its extent, if known, is given as a 5 km section, for example.

Adjacent areas of interest which have often been listed separately in the past are generally combined in this report so that a lake and particularly interesting areas around its shore are found together even if they are not as important as each other. The largest unit is listed first with the total area of all the sites and the subsidary sites are indented below it, each with its areas and importance. Where sites lie in two or more counties they will be found listed in each of them.

3.   Habitat Classification

The purpose of this column for the ecological sites is to indicate the major habitat of interest, the one for which the site would be visited in preference to others. It does not aim at giving a complete list of habitats nor even the most prevalent one, since this information will be found in the site description. A lake, for example, may be included for the marshes that surround it, rather than for the water area itself.

The number of habitat types has been kept to a minimum to avoid confusion. The reader interested in standing water does not therefore have to look up the several categories of lake, pond and reservoir to find sites to visit. The description usually amplifies the habitat type; whether, for example, the lake is temporary or permanent, rich or poor, acid or alkaline. It has been found necessary to use sixteen habitat types, as follows:-

(1) <u>Lake</u> refers to a body of standing water of any size, whether natural or artificial. Where the water is brackish this is indicated by (s).

(2) <u>River</u> includes water moving at any speed whether in a canal, an ordinary channel or a waterfall. It may also be tidal which is indicated by (s).

(3) <u>Sea inlet</u>. A bay of normal salinity, with or without small inflowing streams.

(4) <u>Mudflats</u> are areas without a continuous plant cover which are submerged by every high tide.

(5) <u>Saltmarsh</u> is the community, generally of herbs (non-woody plants) which is covered by high tides at some stage of the tidal cycle but not by all tides.

(6) <u>Marsh</u> is semi-aquatic vegetation growing in an inorganic soil, with stones, silt or clay. It may sometimes be brackish, for example in coastal lagoons, and then it is termed marsh (s).

(7) <u>Fen</u> is the same vegetation type but it is rooted in an organic peat soil which may be alkaline to slightly acidic in nature. The soil is in contact with ground water: it can even be a floating mat of living and dead vegetation over a lake.

(8) <u>Raised bog</u>. A strongly acidic community, usually with <u>Sphagnum</u> moss and scattered dwarf shrubs growing on peat and raised slightly above the general level of the surroundings. The plant cover is above the influence of ground-water and depends largely on rainfall.

(9) <u>Blanket bog</u>. A similar vegetation type which develops on flat or sloping land subject to a large and frequent rainfall (more than 125 cm per annum). It is characteristic of the western seaboard and mountain areas throughout the country.

(10) <u>Heath</u> is restricted mostly to well-drained areas on rock or sand where low shrubs, especially heather and gorse, form a distinctive community.

(11) <u>Exposed rock</u> occurs on cliffs, limestone pavement and on the seashore. If the community is covered by the tide, exposed rock(s) is used.

Many of the marine sites will be found under this
heading if the rocks rather than the sea itself
provide the interesting habitat.

(12) Shingle is a deposit of stones or fine pebbles,
usually on the seashore.

(13) Sand dunes refers to the front section of the
dune system, including embryo dunes and all other
areas dominated by the coarse maritime grasses,
marram, Ammophila, or sea-lyme, Leymus.

(14) Grassland is the community of broad-leaved herbs
and grasses which develops under a wide range of
conditions. It varies much in composition with
acidity, altitude and wetness. It includes the
plantain swards of the west coast which are subject
to sea spray, indicated by grassland(s), and the
callows along the larger rivers. In some cases
grasses form quite a small proportion of the
vegetation, e.g., on exposed limestone and calcareous
dunes.

(15) Turlough. One type of grassland has been separated
out as it also occurs in these distinctive shallow
depressions in the limestone which flood irregularly,
depending on rainfall.

(16) Woodland is divided into deciduous(d), coniferous(c),
and mixed(m) stands. The category includes
those immature or poorly grown examples sometimes
called scrub.

4. Interest

This column gives an indication of the main value of
the site whether it is based on living organisms
(ecological), rocks (geological) or landform
(geomorphological) or a combination of the three.
These interests are listed alphabetically and where
there is the necessary information, ecological sites
are further divided into those with particular
botanical (B), ornithological (O), or zoological (Z),
features. The Irish flora and bird life are much
better known than the rest of the fauna which is
generally more difficult to work on. Thus there is a
bias towards botanical and ornithological sites
and although these life forms are generally quite
good indicators of ecological interest, there are
clearly too few sites of zoological interest to provide
adequate representation of the invertebrate fauna.

Where no specific features stand out, the interest is
labelled simply ecological. Such a site is usually
a good example of a habitat type, such as an oakwood or
a raised bog and is of interest to all biological
disciplines.

5. Description of Site

The description is meant to convey a broad picture of the character of the site, stressing any features of particular interest. It cannot be complete in the small space available. It is written in note form with a number of shorthand conventions. English names of organisms, other than birds and mammals, are often misleading so the standard latin name has generally been added to give clarity. The trees are an exception as their names are widely known. For other organisms the genus name alone has been used when only one species occurs in Ireland, for example, heather Calluna, while the specific name has been added if two or more species are found, e.g., the bell heather Erica cinerea.

In expressing bird numbers there are additional abbreviations. For wintering wildfowl the average peak count is generally given in brackets after the species. There will be many occasions when this maximum is not reached and the words 'up to' should be understood. Similarly, at seabird breeding colonies the numbers given are those proved to breed and the words 'at least' should be added, especially for the nocturnal shearwaters and petrels whose numbers are so difficult to assess. In keeping with current practice some of the nesting auks are given as individuals rather than pairs when numbers on the cliffs vary much throughout the day and no nest is built.

It has been decided not to quote references to the site information contained in this report since they would make the descriptions unnecessarily cumbersome. A list of references would perforce be selective in its treatment of different groups. Nevertheless, a list of general references is appended which will be a guide to the literature and also will give background information to many of the statements made.

3. SUMMARY OF RESULTS

One thousand and fifty-nine separate areas of scientific interest are included in this report (Table 1). Together they cover 231,500 ha of land which is roughly 3 per cent of the area of the country, including tidal mudflats. In absolute terms there are more sites in Galway and fewer in Carlow than in any other county but if the actual size of the areas is taken into account it is seen that Louth and Wicklow come top of the list because of their coastal habitats, followed by Mayo because of its bogland and lakes.

Many of the most important sites are located in the west of the country where the relative warmth of the climate, the mountains and the low density of population combine to produce the most distinctive and best-developed features of the natural heritage. But there is a great deal of interest also in Wexford and Wicklow and, in the Midlands, in Offaly and Westmeath. In fact every county has at least one site of national importance. It may be noticed that the number of sites of local importance does not exceed that of regional sites by as much as would be expected from the use of a four-point scale. This results largely from the lack of geological sites of a local grade. Practically every exposure of rock is of value in elucidating the geology of an area and it became impractical to separate out those of particular importance in the local context without an immense amount of work. This also applies to some extent to ecological sites, particularly in the less-widely known parts of the country.

It must be emphasised that this is only a first attempt at a complete list of areas of scientific interest. Work currently in progress and in the future will undoubtedly yield more sites of importance and necessitate a re-evaluation of those already included.

TABLE 1: <u>Numbers and size of areas of scientific interest in each county.</u>

	International	National	Regional	Local	Total	% of County area
Carlow	-	1	7	9	17	0.83
Cavan	1	2	5	17	25	6.08
Clare	8	13	21	23	65	1.65
Cork	8	10	16	26	60	0.99
Donegal	8	12	31	29	80	3.54
Dublin	3	7	11	13	34	3.27
Galway	7	20	31	26	84	4.51
Kerry	11	14	21	23	69	4.07
Kildare	1	4	6	16	27	3.04
Kilkenny	1	2	10	9	22	0.54
Laois	-	2	11	17	30	2.15
Leitrim	2	1	7	15	25	2.29
Limerick	-	7	15	9	31	0.72
Longford	-	4	2	13	19	5.73
Louth	2	4	6	13	25	8.86
Mayo	8	11	28	27	74	6.64
Meath	1	5	16	18	40	5.72
Monaghan	-	1	7	16	24	1.76
Offaly	3	3	15	14	35	3.24
Roscommon	1	6	11	15	33	4.09
Sligo	2	11	13	13	39	5.72
N. Tipperary	1	2	10	8	21	2.00
S. Tipperary	1	3	12	11	27	0.78
Waterford	-	7	17	13	37	2.14
Westmeath	2	7	7	9	25	5.63
Wexford	7	8	8	12	35	2.93
Wicklow	2	14	21	19	56	8.81
	80	181	365	433	1059	3.28

4. THE USE OF SITES

While the purpose of this report is to encourage an awareness
and appreciation of the national heritage and to direct people's
attention to interesting areas, it must be emphasised not only
that these are often on private land but that they may be
damaged by the visitor himself. The following code of practice
gives guidelines that may be useful.

1. Picking flowers and collecting animals disrupts the natural
   community, it removes the attraction of an area for other
   people and, in some cases, it is illegal under regulations
   imposed by the Wildlife Act, 1976. Collect only if you
   will subsequently use the specimens and then sparingly.

2. Trampling is often done inadvertently, even in the course
   of study. Take care when photographing plants that you
   do not destroy others nearby. Do not walk in moss
   cushions or other soft vegetation where footprints may
   last for three years.

3. Disturbance is an insidious form of damage, the effects of
   which last long after the incident. Take particular care
   where birds or animals are breeding or hibernating, even if
   you are interested in something else. Leave bark on dead
   trees and turn back stones under which you have looked.

4. Never collect geological specimens out of habit, only when
   you are going to extract more information from them and
   then with full details of locality and position. Thought-
   less hammering may damage a unique exposure and ruin the
   site for further research. In particular, do not try to
   remove fossils from flat areas of rock: they will
   probably break.

County Lists of Areas

Name of Area	Habitat	Interest	Description

CARLOW

National importance

Name of Area	Habitat	Interest	Description
1. Slieve Bawn S 81 54 185 ha	Heath	Ecological	An excellent example of stony wet heath with limited peat development. The flora includes the heathers, _Calluna_, _Erica cinerea_ and _E. tetralix_, the autumn gorse, _Ulex gallii_ and much moor grass, _Molinia._ The area shows the finest development of comparatively dry heath in Irish uplands as such sites have elsewhere been covered by blanket bog.

Regional importance

Name of Area	Habitat	Interest	Description
2. Ardristan S 83 70 38 ha	Fen	Ecological (B)	Calcareous swamp and fen with large area of reed, _Phragmites_, and some alder trees at the edge. An interesting flora of sedges and orchids occurs. Diverse invertebrate populations and visiting waterfowl.
3. Bagenalstown esker S 72 62 85 ha	Grassland	Geomorpho-logical Ecological	Long glacial hill of water-sorted sand and gravel. Quarrying is extensive and only the northern section is still intact. It has a well-developed calcareous grassland community.
4. Baggot's Wood S 93 82 12 ha	Woodland (d)	Ecological	Mixed coniferous and oak wood with hazel and holly. Typical acid woodland ground flora. Small marsh at foot of southern slope adds diversity to site.
5. Bahana & Drummond Wood S 72 40 & 73 36 15 ha	Woodland (d)	Ecological (B)	Scattered patches of deciduous woodland occur amongst coniferous plantations on the valley side of the Barrow river. Oak, holly and bramble in south; beech and elder in north. The white-beam, _Sorbus devoniensis_, occurs.
6. Borris Estate S 72 50 92 ha	Woodland (d)	Ecological	One of the largest deciduous woods in the county. Predominantly oak with hazel, beech and holly. Characteristic ground flora, including elements from wet clay soils, e.g. bugle, _Ajuga reptans_, and the sedge, _Carex strigosa._ Diversity of pass-erine birds occurs with a typical woodland insect fauna.
7. Carrickduff & Coolaphuca S 91 57 92 ha	Woodland (d)	Ecological (B)	Together, these woods form the largest deciduous stand in the county. The main species is oak with some beech, birch and hazel. There is little regeneration except by beech. A diverse herb flora occurs, including several species characteristic of old woodland. Passerine birds numerous and of many species.
8. Killeshin Glen S 661 773 2 ha	-	Geological	A valuable stream section through Upper Namurian fossiliferous rocks in which goniatites are frequent.

Local importance

Name of Area	Habitat	Interest	Description
9. Ballyteigelea S 714 517 1 ha	Woodland (d)	Ecological	A small hazel coppice north-west of Borris, the remnant of a formerly more extensive area. Also in the scrub are birch, willow and hawthorn. Characteristic woodland ground flora.

Name of Area	Habitat	Interest	Description
CARLOW			
Local importance			
10. Carrig Beg S 747 602 2 ha	Marsh	Ecological	This is a small swamp near Ballinakill dominated by clubrush, Scirpus lacustris, at the western end. It has a small water bird population.
11. Cloughristick Wood S 70 69 10 ha	Woodland (d)	Ecological	Woodland set on the flood plain of the river Barrow. Predominant tree species is willow with oak and beech. Hazel is abundant and coniferous species occur. Rich herb flora, characteristic of wetland and woodland habitats.
12. Kilcarry Wood S 89 61 10 ha	Woodland (d)	Ecological	Hazel scrub on eastern side of Slaney valley with other deciduous trees.
13. Oakpark S 74 80 18 ha	Lake Woodland (d)	Ecological (O)	Shallow, artificial pond with much reed, Phragmites, surrounded by woodland. Largest area of standing water in the county supporting over half of its wintering wildfowl. Even-aged oak woodland with understorey of hazel and typical ground flora being replaced by rhododendron.
14. Pollymounty River valley S 74 35 19 ha	Grassland	Ecological (B)	Tributary valley and flood plain of the River Barrow. Hazel and willow occur on the steep slopes, mixed in with coniferous plantations. Rich variety of mosses and liverworts. Wet grassland includes strawberry clover, Trifolium fragiferum.
15. Slaney valley S 87 67 150 ha	Woodland (d)	Ecological	Woodland set on the sides of a deeply cut valley between Aghade and Kilcarry. Extensive areas of hazel and oak with taller oak trees and coniferous species. Holly and a typical ground flora occur.
16. St. Mullin's Red Bog S 73 38 14 ha	Raised bog	Ecological (B)	Partially cutover raised bog with sufficient wet ground for the more unusual plant species of this habitat e.g. cranberry, Vaccinium oxycoccus. Small stands of birch and abundant lichens on dry peat.
17. Tullow ponds S 839 721 3 ha	Lake	Ecological (B)	A series of shallow ponds, including Doyle's Pond and Lough Martin, subject to periodic flooding. A wildfowl habitat of local importance only. The sedge, Carex vesicaria, has been recorded.

Name of Area	Habitat	Interest	Description

CAVAN

International importance

| 1. | Lough Oughter
H 34 05
8900 ha | Lake
Woodland (d) | Ecological (B,O) | The best inland example of a flooded drumlin landscape with rich and varied aquatic plant communities. Internationally important flocks of whooper swan (560) winter on the lough and the largest concentration of breeding great crested grebes in the Republic occurs here. The invertebrate fauna is well-developed. The area includes old estate woodlands usually established on poorly drained clayey soils. Both the shrub and ground floras contain many species of interest. |

National importance

| 2. | Lough Cratty
H 15 27
500 ha | Blanket bog | Ecological | Relatively undisturbed blanket bog which is unusual for its size and naturalness. The diversity and range of plant species and lichens is high and the bog is actively growing through the agency of large Sphagnum cushions. |
| 3. | Lough Kinale
& Derragh
Lough
N 39 82
40 ha
(also in
Longford &
Westmeath) | Lake | Ecological (O) | A highly productive lake, rich in invertebrates which support a large wildfowl population and considerable numbers of migrating waders (see Longford for details). The plant communities around the lake margin contain a variety of species typical of base-rich marshes. |

Regional importance

4.	Bruse Hill N 31 98 110 ha	Heath Marsh	Ecological (B)	Typical upland grassland alternates with drier heath communities and wet flushes dominated by sedges. High floral diversity with some uncommon species. Larger fauna includes the lizard in rocky sites.
5.	Clonty Lough H 27 12 34 ha	Fen	Ecological (B)	Calcareous lake surrounded in places by dense reedswamp merging into a more mineral marsh, which dries substantially in summer. Vegetation typical of these habitats except for a large proportion of the uncommon sedge, Carex elongata. Lakeside vegetation provides rich feeding for a wide variety of birds.
6.	Corratirrim H 07 37 150 ha	Exposed rock	Ecological	The area includes limestone pavement, small cliffs, grassland and patches of hazel scrub, habitats which do not occur together elsewhere in the county. The flora is generally species-rich though not as well-developed as on the Connaught limestones. Caves and subterranean drainage are both frequent.
7.	Pollahune H 0892 3205 1.5 km section	-	Geomorphological	An extensive cave system with 1.5 km of major stream passages. The water has been shown to flow into the Shannon Pot about 4 km to the west.
8.	Shannon Pot H 0533 3176 1 ha	-	Geomorphological	The recognised source of the Shannon where the overground river begins its course in a pool 9.5 m deep. This collects water from a much wider area.

Name of Area	Principal Habitat(s)	Interest	Description
CAVAN			
Local importance			
9. Annagh Lough H 29 18 63 ha	Lake	Ecological (B)	Base-rich lake with peat bog and woodland provides a rich flora and insect life. The lake supports a variety of coarse fish; also stocked with brown trout. Small numbers of wintering wildfowl.
10. Bellavally Mountain H 11 22 80 ha	Blanket bog	Ecological	Variety of interesting plants on cliff south of Bellavally Gap. To the south-west a typical blanket bog shows the first stages of erosion.
11. Blackrock's Cross H 15 23 16 ha	Blanket bog	Ecological	Blanket bog on upper slopes and wet acidic grassland on lower ground. Trees and shrubs re-establishing themselves in some areas. Fast-flowing unpolluted stream. Rich insect and bird faunas.
12. Cloghbally Bog N 68 83 174 ha	Raised bog	Ecological	Best example of a raised bog in the county with typical and relatively undisturbed flora.
13. Cordonaghy Bog N 31 95 74 ha	Raised bog Fen	Ecological (B)	Cut-over bog with a diversity of plant communities, including sedges and ferns of interest.
14. Drumkeen House woodland H 41 07 17 ha	Woodland (d)	Ecological	Planted beech, sycamore, elm and oak with typical ground flora and characteristic bird species, including jay and woodcock.
15. Farren Connell Estate N 49 82 140 ha	Woodland (d) Raised bog	Ecological	Mainly beech, oak, sycamore, lime and horse-chesnut with some pines and firs situated on the remnants of a raised bog. Unplanted north-east section supports a typical bog flora. Many different communities of the woodland/bogland transition occur with a fairly rich animal life in the woodland.
16. Glasshouse Lough H 28 06 85 ha	Marsh	Ecological (B)	Small lake with several areas of woodland growing along the shore. Typical woodland ground flora with a rich variety of herbs. Stony area surrounding lake supports many sedges and mosses. Several species of wading birds breed in the area.
17. Lough Gowna N 28 89 377 ha (also in Longford)	Lake	Ecological (B,O)	A shallow lake set amongst drumlins on the river Erne system. It has a relatively low base status which allows aquatic plants such as Lobelia, and quillwort, Isoetes lacustris, to grow in a pH of 7.5. The lake holds small populations of wildfowl in winter, especially wigeon (360), goldeneye (50) and wild swan (60) but is perhaps more important as a breeding area for wildfowl, grebes and gulls. A woodland fringe covers part of the shore with willow, ash and sometimes oak.
18. Lough Macnean Upper H 04 37 195 ha	Heath	Ecological	A heath community occurs around much of this limestone lake with scattered shrubs and trees and wet grassland on the lower shores. Plants on the lake edge include northern bedstraw, Galium boreale.

Name of Area	Habitat	Interest	Description

Local importance

Name of Area	Habitat	Interest	Description
19. Lough Ramor N 60 80 750 ha	Lake	Ecological (B)	Nutritionally a poor lake, bordered by alder, willow and hazel woodland which supports a variety of birds. Islands are covered by willows and used by breeding wildfowl and gulls. Lakeside marshes have many sedges along with a wide range of other plants e.g. bur marigolds, *Bidens* spp. and the spearwort, *Ranunculus lingua*.
20. Lough Sheelin shore N 47 85 5 km section	Marsh	Ecological	Calcareous grassland and marshes cover much of the shore with some acid flushing from raised bogs nearby. The area supports a variety of breeding wildfowl, waders and passerines.
21. Madabawn H 64 09 13 ha	Marsh	Ecological	A small marsh and floating fen with limited vegetation but some interesting plants. It supports an abundance of several dragonfly species.
22. Moneenterriff cliffs H 03 25 33 ha	Exposed rock	Ecological (Z)	Greatest expanse of cliffs and block scree in the county supporting a variety of plant communities and providing habitats for invertebrates, birds and mammals.
23. Peartree Lake H 40 80 4 ha	Lake	Ecological (Z)	The lake has an unusual fish population holding first and second generation roach, bream and rudd hybrids.
24. Polladrossan H 0627 3527 0.5 km section	–	Geological Geomorphological	A cave that includes 500 m of dry passages and streams. It also has some features of geological interest.
25. St Augustine's Caves H 0527 3754 0.5 km section	–	Geomorphological	A small cave system that is easy of access. 300 m of well-decorated stream passages occur.

Name of Area	Habitat	Interest	Description

CLARE

International importance

1. **Black Head**
M 14 11
790 ha
Habitat: Grassland, Exposed rock, Heath
Interest: Ecological (B), Geomorphological
Description: The area encompasses a complete range of rocky Burren habitats from coastal, glacially-planed limestone pavement to high level heaths with bearberry, Arctostaphylos. It supports a large variety of interesting plants, such as the saxifrages, S. rosacea and S. hypnoides, and mountain avens, Dryas.

2. **Fisherstreet**
R 060 957
1.5 km section
Habitat: -
Interest: Geological
Description: A coastal section with a remarkable development of sand volcanoes in Carboniferous beds overlying slumped shales and sandstones.

3. **Lurga Point to Spanish Point**
R 00 75
69 ha
Habitat: Exposed rock(s)
Interest: Ecological
Description: The limestone coastline supports a very rich development of sublittoral communities, containing a particularly good variety of red algae. The sea urchin, Paracentrotus, and the mussel, Mytillus, are characteristic of the intertidal zone.

4. **Mullagh More**
R 31 94
560 ha
Habitat: Grassland, Woodland(d), Exposed rock, Turlough
Interest: Ecological (B,Z), Geological
Description: One of the centres of development of the Burren flora with species-rich communities occurring in a wide range of habitats. Small patches of woodland (with elm), extensive limestone pavements and several turloughs are included. The invertebrate fauna is also rich. Some of the only folding of Carboniferous limestone in the Burren is seen in the hill itself.

5. **Pol-an-Ionain**
M 105 004
0.5 km section
Habitat: -
Interest: Geological
Description: A small cave system ending in a large chamber with extensive mud deposits. One of the largest stalactites in the world (10 m long) hangs from the roof of this chamber.

6. **Poulnagollum-Poulelva**
M 161 038
11 km section
Habitat: -
Interest: Geological
Description: This is the longest cave system in the country, consisting of classical canyon passageways with well-developed rock features. The large pot-hole entrance occurs further from the edge of the overlying shales than most others.

7. **Poulsallagh**
M 08 02
195 ha
Habitat: Exposed rock(s), Grassland
Interest: Ecological (B), Geomorphological
Description: Characteristic Burren communities occur here beside the coast road, locally modified by the maritime conditions. They include a high density of the more interesting species whose origins vary from Arctic regions to the Mediterranean. Limestone scarps and block moraine provide a diversity of habitats. Coastal cliffs and littoral areas are also of value.

8. **River Fergus Estuary**
R 35 70
650 ha
Habitat: Mudflats
Interest: Ecological (O)
Description: The most important section of the Shannon Estuary with a varied saltmarsh and maritime flora. Rich in invertebrates which serve as food for many thousands of wintering waders and duck. Black-tailed godwit (6,600), redshank (1,700), dunlin (14,800) and wigeon (4,300) are the main species in winter; these numbers are all of international importance. Shoveler, scaup and greylag goose populations are also of note.

Name of Area	Habitat	Interest	Description

CLARE

National importance

9. Ballyallia Lough
R 34 81
35 ha
— Lake — Ecological (B,O) — Small lake on the river Fergus with an unusual aquatic plant, the hornwort, _Cerato-phyllum_. The lake and surrounding grassland are important for wintering wildfowl and waders. Shoveler (500) and gadwall (100) occur in numbers of national significance. This represents about 20 % of gadwall wintering in Ireland. Large flocks of common species also are present, e.g. mallard (300), teal (600), wigeon (1,800) and black-tailed godwit (100).

10. Ballyeighter Loughs
R 34 92
520 ha
— Fen, Lake — Ecological — A large area of fen and calcareous marsh occurs around this indented lake, especially at the south-western end. The fen flora is well-developed with large areas of saw sedge, _Cladium_, and bog-rush, _Schoenus_, with a full complement of associated species. A rich fauna also occurs.

11. Cliffs of Moher
R 03 91
150 ha
— Exposed rock, Grassland — Ecological (B,O), Geomorphological — Vertical sea cliffs in Upper Carboniferous shales and flagstones, this area is of considerable amenity value. It bears a characteristic maritime flora with some unusual features and the largest colonies of seabirds in the county. Nationally important for razorbill (2,800), guillemot (12,800) and puffin (1,360). Other nesting species include kittiwake (4,700 prs), fulmar (2,200 prs), herring gull (500 prs), great black-backed gull (20 prs), shag (20 prs), chough and rock dove. Three cliff faces are used in an annual census to monitor seabird populations.

12. Cullaun caves
M 195 018
8.7 km section
— - — Geomorphological — The two caves Cullaun III and IV/V are treated together having passages of 3.6 and 5.1 km respectively. The first is a very well-decorated system, some of which floods frequently. Cullaun IV/V has an interesting hydrology related to the overlying shale and structural features in the rock.

13. Doolin - St. Catherine's Cave
R 075 969
6.4 km section
— - — Geomorphological — A very extensive cave system with a major stream passage passing under a surface river and ending on the foreshore in a tidal sump.

14. Fanore dunes
M 13 08
30 ha
— Grassland, Sand dunes — Ecological (B,Z) — The best developed and most interesting sand dune system in the county with the hollows between the dunes sometimes showing limestone pavement. A varied flora occurs with unusual grassland communities and an interesting invertebrate fauna.

15. Glenomera Wood
R 61 67
30 ha
— Woodland (d) — Ecological — Sessile oakwood regenerating naturally amongst dense holly and birch with a sparse ground flora, at least at this stage. Conditions favour pheasant, woodcock and many passerine birds.

16. Lough Bunny
R 37 96
125 ha
— Fen, Grassland, Lake — Ecological (B,O) — A deep lake with aquatic vegetation confined to sheltered bays and inlets. Fen areas are well-developed and include many orchid species. Elsewhere limestone outcrops support the full range of the Burren flora with dropwort, _Filipendula vulgaris,_ and a good variety of shrubby species. The western shore is partly peat-covered with more typical plant communities. Regular haunt for wildfowl and waders with cormorant, black-headed gull and terns present in summer.

Name of Area	Habitat	Interest	Description

CLARE

National importance

17.	Mutton Island Q 97 74 40 ha	Grassland	Ecological (O) Geomorphological	Important for wintering wildfowl particularly barnacle geese (500), teal (150) mallard (50) and gadwall (20). A few breeding seabirds occur together with a large population of hares. The south Irish end moraine crosses the island and is easily seen.
18.	Poulavallan & Glen of Clab M 29 O2 20 ha	Woodland (d)	Ecological Geomorphological	A depression (doline) which occasionally floods and a dry valley, both with much woodland. This is dominated by hazel and ash, with rowan, birch and goat willow. A rich ground flora is present with an abundance of ferns and mosses. Some of the best developed woodland in the Burren.
19.	Roadford R 082 970 1 ha	-	Geological	In the river about 1 km above Roadford, an outcrop of rock phosphate occurs at the base of the Namurian.
20.	Shannon Airport shore R 37 59 380 ha	Mudflats Lake (s)	Ecological (O)	Totals of 3,300 wildfowl and 20,000 waders in winter include large numbers of godwits (black-tailed 4,900, bar-tailed 1,200), knot (2,500), dunlin (7,000) and dabbling duck. Saltmarsh at Rineanna Point is of interest also.
21.	Tullaher Lough Q 95 61 88 ha	Blanket bog	Ecological (B,O)	Diverse aquatic and bog flora and fauna including several plant species characteristic of Atlantic regions. Used by small numbers of wintering duck (250), white-fronted geese (50) and snipe.

Regional importance

22.	Abbey Hill M 30 10 70 ha (also in Galway)	-	Geomorphological	A major scarp feature, forming the north-east boundary to the Burren hills.
23.	Ailwee cave M 237 044 0.5 km	-	Geological	A recently discovered cave now developed and open to the public. Some animal remains from Postglacial times have been found here.
24.	Ballycar Lough R 41 68 18 ha	Fen	Ecological (B)	Reedswamp occurs on the north and west sides, grazing land to the south. The northern limb is overgrown by a mat of sedges and here, bog vegetation is invading the fen community. Two plant species are present that are fairly rare in Clare.
25.	Ballycullinan Lake R 29 85 33 ha	Lake	Ecological (B)	Important for an alga, _Cladophora sauteri_, which has been observed only in three other Irish localities. It forms spherical bodies called 'moor balls' apparently from being rolled around on the bottom.
26.	Ballymihill cave M 247 018 0.5 km section	-	Geological	The cave is of interest since its sediments contain the remains of woodland snails and hardwood charcoal.
27.	Ballyvaughan saltmarsh M 21 09 140 ha	Saltmarsh	Ecological	A small, but interesting saltmarsh occurs on this site, locally important for wintering waders and wildfowl, particularly brent geese.

Name of Area	Habitat	Interest	Description
CLARE			
Regional importance			
28. Ballyvaughan turlough M 220 080 9 ha	Turlough	Ecological (B)	One of the best developed stands of shrubby cinquefoil, _Potentilla fruticosa_, in Ireland. Otherwise, it has a typical turlough flora.
29. Bridges of Ross Q 73 50 10 ha	-	Geomorphological	Wave erosion on this section of the coast has produced a good series of natural arches, caves and other features.
30. Cahermurphy (L. Graney) R 57 92 24 ha	Woodland (d)	Ecological	Two woodlands of interest occur on the east side of L. Graney. At Cahermurphy, the intact oak-wood has a good structure and ground communities. A similar community near Knockbeha Cottage has been felled but woodland is regenerating well with some oak and much birch and holly. The former site is a Nature Reserve.
31. Clonderalaw Bay R 12 53 75 ha	Mudflats	Ecological (O)	Large numbers of shorebirds are present in autumn and winter; wildfowl (1,400) are mostly wigeon, waders (2,200) include many species.
32. Coskeam cave M 311 017 0.5 km section	-	Geological	This system includes interesting solution features of great age which developed below the water table of the period.
33. Craglea quarry R 688 756 2 ha	-	Geological	A quarry section showing features of the Slieve Bernagh inlier. It is the type locality for some of the local rocks.
34. Derrymore Wood R 42 84 14 ha	Woodland (d)	Ecological	An almost pure oak/holly woodland with some birch and hazel. The ground flora is typical of western oakwood with good development of lower plants.
35. Doonyvarden cave M 294 016 1 km section	-	Geological	Deposition and other features are well-developed in this cave system which also has an interesting hydrology.
36. Dromoland Lake R 39 70 16 ha	Fen	Ecological (B)	Supports a diverse flora and fauna, somewhat resembling that of the Burren. Plants include a number of uncommon sedges, especially _Carex appropinquata_, which has here its only station in the county.
37. Inchicronan Lough R 39 86 65 ha	Grassland	Ecological (B)	The area contains interesting lake and fen communities, including common meadow-rue, _Thalictrum flavum_, a plant of the central plain. The calcicole/calcifuge transition is of ecological interest.
38. Knockauns Mountain M 12 04 40 ha	-	Geological Geomorpholigical	The boundary between the soft shales and the harder but soluble limestone creates striking differences in topography, drainage and vegetation. Sink holes and caves are frequent.
39. Lough Atedaun R 29 88 81 ha	Lake	Ecological (O)	A limestone lake with aquatic vegetation and grassland attractive to whooper (100) and Bewick's (100) swans and wigeon (3,000). Used also by waders.

Name of Area	Habitat	Interest	Description

CLARE

Regional importance

40. Loop Head
Q 68 96
160 ha

Grassland(s)
Exposed rock

Ecological(B,O)

Typical maritime plant communities occur, including the plantain sward which is characteristic of exposed parts of the west coast. Fairly large numbers of nesting seabirds, mainly kittiwake (435 prs) and guillemot (2,600).

41. Poulnasherry
Bay
R 94 57
570 ha

Mudflats

Ecological (O)

Diversity of habitats makes this an important wintering site for wildfowl. Estuary includes stony and muddy sections, also cord-grass, Spartina, stands. Average population of 2,000 wildfowl includes brent geese (300), wigeon (1,000) and teal (500). Wader numbers vary up to 3,000.

42. Slieve Carran
woods
M 32 03
66 ha

Woodland (d)

Ecological

One of the most natural tracts of woodland in the Burren, consisting of hazel, ash, rowan and spindle with a diverse ground flora. Well-developed bird fauna.

Local importance

43. Ballyeighter
wood
R 34 93
12 ha

Woodland (d)

Ecological

Unusual scrub community on limestone with regenerating oak amongst the hazel, holly and hawthorn.

44. Ballyogan
Lough
R 37 90
63 ha

Fen
Raised bog

Ecological (B)

Shallow peat has developed on pure calcareous marl, giving rise to acidic plant communities in a predominantly alkaline area. The peat community is dominated by bog rush, Schoenus, moor grass, Molinia, and in places by Sphagnum moss.

45. Bouleevin
M 34 01
52 ha

Woodland (d)

Ecological

An open birch/hazel community which is rare on limestone.

46. Cahircalla
R 310 750
9 ha

Woodland (d)

Ecological

Predominantly a young ash wood with hawthorn, hazel, sycamore, birch, beech and blackthorn. A rich herb flora occurs, containing most characteristic woodland plants. Large and varied passerine bird fauna.

47. Caher River
M 16 07
6 km section

River

Ecological (B)

An interesting aquatic flora occurs along the course of the river - the only permanent above-ground one in the Burren.

48. Cahiracon
wood
R 228 543
5 ha

Woodland (d)

Ecological

Narrow fringe of oakwood along the shore of the Shannon Estuary with both calcifuge and calcicole plant species growing in it.

49. Carran
depression
R 29 98
90 ha

Turlough
Fen

Ecological (O)
Geomorphological

A depression caused by the collapse of under-lying caves. Turlough habitat at 115 m O.D., the highest in the country. Fen communities adjacent to permanent ponds. Pochard (125) and small numbers of other duck are present in winter. Roost for white-fronted geese.

50. Cloonamirran
wood
R 72 87
10 ha

Woodland (d)

Ecological

Blanket bog being colonised by holly and birch with a few oaks and planted beech. Simple ground flora more typical of blanket bog than of woodland. A good example of ecological succession.

51. Cloonsneachta
Lough
R 215 594
8 ha

Lake

Ecological (Z)

An acid stony lake with limited vegetation. The fish fauna includes a race of char. The lake is surrounded by acid grassland and patches of bog.

Name of Area	Habitat	Interest	Description

CLARE

Local importance

52. Derryhumma wood R 428 850 6 ha	Woodland(d)	Ecological	Remnants of natural oakwood are regenerating freely and invading the surrounding areas, including a wet birchwood. Willow, holly and a typical calcifuge ground flora are also present.
53. Dromore Lough R 35 75 39 ha	Lake Fen	Ecological	A calcareous east Clare lake with an interesting ecology. There are complete transitions from aquatic to woodland communities including coniferous woods on parts of the shore. The fauna is of particular interest, both vertebrate and invertebrate.
54. Faunarooska M 141 050 1.7 km section	-	Geomorphological	An unusual cave in that it descends steeply to about 95 m below the entrance. Chert bands bridge the canyon passage in places and accumulations of soil occur in the lower reaches.
55. Fin Lough R 43 69 80 ha	Lake	Ecological (Z)	Typical east Clare lough on limestone used by small numbers of wintering wildfowl. An unusual insect fauna is also present.
56. Garrannon wood R 49 60 22 ha	Woodland (d)	Ecological	An almost pure stand of managed oak with some birch, alder and hawthorn towards the east. Insect fauna well-developed.
57. Illaunonearaun Q 830 570 1 ha	Grassland (s)	Ecological (O)	A wintering area for barnacle geese (90) and breeding site for gulls, especially the great black-backed (100 prs).
58. Inchiquin Lough R 26 89 40 ha	Lake Marsh	Ecological	Woodland on west side contains planted sycamore and beech and many native species. The shore-line vegetation at the north end is of some interest. Small numbers of duck and coot use the lake in winter and it apparently has the highest natural stocking rate of wild brown trout in the country.
59. Kilcorney caves R 226 991 0.5 km section	-	Gemorphological	A series of semi-active and active caves, some of which are associated with a turlough. Kilcorney is known as the cave of the wild horses.
60. Lough Donnell R 00 71 68 ha	Lake(s)	Ecological	A lake near Quilty impounded by a large storm beach of rounded stones. It is used by small numbers of wintering wildfowl and waders.
61. Lough Murree & Finavarra M 26 11 44 ha	Exposed rock(s) Lake (s)	Ecological	Aquatic flora dominated by pondweeds with a rare charophyte, Lamprothamnion sp. Important wintering resort for pochard and, occasionally, other waterbirds. Supports a rich invertebrate fauna. The seashore has well-developed algal communities which have been the subject of considerable research.
62. Mattle Island Q 975 720 1 ha	Exposed rock	Ecological (O)	Seabird colony with breeding cormorant (80 prs) and shag (20 prs); also some gulls (200 prs).

Name of Area	Habitat	Inerest	Description

CLARE

Local importance

63.	Rinskea shore R 782 900 5 ha	Heath	Ecological	Part of the Lough Derg shoreline dominated by a heathy association of gorse and juniper. Herbaceous plants include bracken, Pteridium, yellow rattle, Rhinanthus, and tormentil, Potentilla erecta.
64.	Scarrif River R 65 83 10 ha	Fen	Ecological (B)	An interesting marsh and fen flora occurs where the river flows into Lough Derg. It includes the stitchwort, Stellaria palustris.
65.	St Senan's Lough R 05 54 11 ha	Fen	Ecological	A shallow acid lake with unusual floating fen community of mosses, especially Polytrichum, at one end. Typical marsh flora also occurs around the lake.

Name of Area	Habitat	Interest	Description
CORK			
International importance			
1. Ballyheedy W 603 601 0.1 ha	–	Geological	An isolated site near an old quarry, which shows the type section for the fossil fish, <u>Rhabdoderma (Coelacanthus) elongatus</u>.
2. Courtmacsherry Bay W 65 43 3.2 km section	–	Geological Geomorphological	Around the bay the rock platform is cut across the highly inclined block-slates and sandstones of the Carboniferous series. This is the type section for the Courtmacsherry raised beach and for the raised marine platform of the south of Ireland.
3. Glengarriff woodland V 92 57 100 ha	Woodland(d)	Ecological	Similar in general aspect to the Killarney oak woodlands. Oak, birch and rowan are common with well-developed understorey of holly and the strawberry tree in unshaded sites. Rich ground flora with filmy ferns, <u>Hymenophyllum</u> spp., and many mosses and liverworts.
4. Gowlane, Castletownbere V 670 495 0.5 ha	–	Geological	Fossil soil showing fine examples of podsolisation. A classic site for soil science.
5. Knockowen Mountain V 81 55 10 ha	Exposed rock	Ecological (B)	Unusual high level community on rocks near summit. Species include a sandwort, <u>Minuartia recurva</u>, an alpine plant unknown elsewhere in Ireland or Britain.
6. Lough Hyne & nearby inlet W 10 29 400 ha	Sea inlet	Ecological (B,Z)	Deep land-locked bay joined to the Atlantic by a very narrow shallow channel, so that tides are reduced to a metre or so. Great diversity and abundance of animal and plant species. Deep water animals occur in shallow water among littoral forms. Studied by marine scientists for many years.
7. Mountgabriel V 92 34 55 ha	–	Geological	Bronze age copper mines, unique because of the lack of later workings. This site is a National Monument.
8. Ringabella Bay & Point W 790 580 1 km section	–	Geomorphological Geological	A low drift cliff sloping down below high water mark and covering a raised platform which has been striated by moving ice. At Ringabella Point there is a small exposure of black pyritous mudstone with interesting goniatite fossils. It is the type locality for one species, unknown elsewhere in western Europe.
National Importance			
9. Ballycroneen Bay W 906 610 1 km section	–	Geological	The type site for a widely occurring till deposited by the Irish Sea glacier.
10. Bantry drumlins V 99 50 400 ha	–	Geomorphological	A small drumlin swarm at the head of Bantry Bay, partially inundated by the sea. It seems to be the only group of drumlins produced by a local mountain glaciation rather than a general ice-sheet.

Plate 1:   An acid mountain river near Glengariff, Co. Cork, with
woodland colonising the hillside behind. This is caused
by a reduction in grazing intensity as sheep and cattle
otherwise remove all tree seedlings. (Cork 3).

Plate 2:   The flowers of pipewort, _Eriocaulon_, an aquatic plant
occurring in many western regions from Donegal to Kerry
and also in North America. Here it is seen growing with
white waterlily, _Nymphaea_; elsewhere water lobelia, _Lobelia_
and bulbous rush, _Juncus bulbosus_, occur. (Donegal 51).

Name of Area	Habitat	Interest	Description

CORK

National importance

11. Ballymacoda
Clonpriest
& Pillmore
W 40 39
640 ha
— Grassland / Mudflats — Ecological (O) — Extensive area of marshy fields, salt-marsh and mudflats. Vegetation on calcareous sands of some interest. Wintering area for waders and wildfowl, including internationally important numbers of golden plover (up to 15,000), lapwing (8,000), black-tailed godwit (2,800) and dunlin (4,200). Wigeon (1,000), curlew (2,500), and bar-tailed godwit (870) also occur.

Name of Area	Habitat	Interest	Description
11. Ballymacoda Clonpriest & Pillmore W 40 39 640 ha	Grassland Mudflats	Ecological (O)	Extensive area of marshy fields, salt-marsh and mudflats. Vegetation on calcareous sands of some interest. Wintering area for waders and wildfowl, including internationally important numbers of golden plover (up to 15,000), lapwing (8,000), black-tailed godwit (2,800) and dunlin (4,200). Wigeon (1,000), curlew (2,500), and bar-tailed godwit (870) also occur.
12. Ballydesmond R 151 042 0.5 ha	–	Geological	A quarry, which exhibits the best example in the country of tundra frost polygons formed during the last glaciation.
13. Black Ball Head V 582 395 2 ha	–	Geological	An exposure of igneous material which has been intruded into the sedimentary country rock. In the cliff section, the sea has eroded into the intrusives, exposing the internal structure.
14. Bull & Cow Rocks V 410 400 9 ha	Exposed rock	Ecological (O)	An important seabird breeding colony. Total numbers in the area include gannet (1,000 prs), storm petrel (1,000 prs), guillemot (2,600) razorbill (1,500 prs), puffin (400 prs), and kittiwake (1,000 prs). The Bull houses the gannet and storm petrel colonies and the majority of the razorbill; the Cow most of the guillemot.
15. Castlepook caves R 615 113 0.7 km section	–	Geological	A limestone cave system formed of canyon passages but at present not fully explored. Remains of the Preglacial fauna have been collected here.
16. Garryvoe W 99 66 77 ha	–	Geomorphological	A high cliff of glacial material which shows the stratigraphic relationship between the local Garryvoe till produced by a mountain ice-sheet and the Ballycroneen till, deposited by the Irish Sea glacier.
17. Great Island Channel W 81 71 900 ha	Mudflats	Ecological (O)	One of the most important areas for wildfowl within Cork Harbour. Shelduck occur in internationally important numbers (1,500 during March) with mallard, wigeon, teal and a substantial wader population, e.g. dunlin (5,000).
18. Old Head of Kinsale W 62 42 10 km section	Exposed rock	Ecological (O) Geological	Important exposures on both sides of headland of sandstones from the Devonian to the Carboniferous. Probably the most complete succession through the Cork beds. Large breeding seabird colonies with kittiwake (1,700 prs), guillemot (2,000) and razorbill (100) the most important species.
19. Tivoli-Dunkettle shore W 72 73 44 ha	Mudflats	Ecological (O)	The largest roost and feeding area for waders in Cork Harbour on the mudflats and newly reclaimed land. Up to 7,000 present during winter, including black-tailed godwit (2,000), bar-tailed godwit (500), dunlin (1,500) and oystercatcher (1,000). Black-tailed godwit numbers are of international importance.

Name of Area	Habitat	Interest	Description

Regional importance

Name of Area	Habitat	Interest	Description
20. Adrigole V 80 49 14 ha	Marsh	Ecological (B)	Plant communities contain several uncommon species including the water crowfoot, _Ranunculus tripartitus_, and the sedge, _Carex punctata_.
21. Ballincollig caves W 806 707	–	Geomorphological	A small limestone cave under the N.E. corner of Ballincollig Castle, in which an assemblage of zoological remains has been found.
22. Ballycotton Bay W 99 65 500 ha	Lake(s)	Ecological (O)	Coastal marsh and lagoons recently cut off from the sea, and saltmarsh communities. Extensive beds of beaked tassel weed, _Zannichellia_. Used by a wide variety of wintering birds. Wildfowl number 800 and include gadwall.
23. Ballyvergan marsh X 09 76 53 ha	Marsh Fen	Ecological (B,O)	An extensive area of reed swamp with very well-developed animal and plant communities. A good example of transition from marsh to scrub occurs in one place. The shrimp, _Neomysis integer_, is abundant.
24. Carrigtwohill caves W 810 730 0.5 km section	–	Geomorphological	A cave system containing fine examples of dripstone formations.
25. Clonakilty Bay W 39 39 650 ha	Mudflats	Ecological (O)	This is the third most important site for waders in the county. At times they have totalled 8,000, including curlew (800), dunlin (1,100) and black-tailed godwit (700).
26. Cloyne esker W 887 673 15 ha	–	Geomorphological	One of the only eskers in Cork whose origin is associated with the Cork/Kerry ice cap.
27. Garrylucas marsh W 61 43 30 ha	Marsh	Ecological (B)	A coastal marsh of considerable ecological interest behind Garristown beach. Such communities are generally rare on the south coast and this is the only station for the marsh fern, _Thelypteris palustris_, for example, between Wicklow and Kerry.
28. Gortmore caves W 445 987 0.6 km section	–	Geological	A series of cave passages including some dry stretches occurs beside the Blackwater at this point. Many characteristic features are developed including straw stalactites. Quarrying has interferred with one of the caves.
29. Kilcolman Bog R 58 11 52 ha	Lake Marsh	Ecological (B,O)	Site of a former lake, now mostly covered over with marsh and fen communities with several uncommon plant species. Open ponds maintained for wildfowl. Important wintering area for dabbling duck, e.g. teal (1,200), wigeon (800), shoveler (350) and whooper swan (20).
30. Knockadoon Head X 29 70 50 ha	–	Geological	A rocky headland, on which the junction between the Carboniferous and Devonian sandstone is exposed on the cliff face. A good sequence of Quaternary sediments and a striated rock platform occur also.
31. Lissagriffin Lake V 77 27 150 ha	Lake(s)	Ecological (O)	The shallow sand-filled lake is firstly a feeding ground for wintering wildfowl and waders and secondly a moulting area for a large flock of mute swan.
32. Loughavaul V 909 531 8.5 ha	Lake	Ecological (Z)	A lake near Glengarriff at 120 m, it has an unusual ecology, supporting fast-growing trout in spite of its acidity.

Name of Area	Habitat	Interest	Description
CORK			
Regional importance			
33. Rock Farm Quarry, Little Island W 76 71 30 ha	Grassland	Ecological (B) Geological	A series of limestone quarries in which the limestone is divided into three distinctive zones of the Visean (Lower Carboniferous). A rich calcicole flora occurs, including dense-flowered orchid, Neotinea.
34. St Gobnet's Wood W 10 78 29 ha	Woodland(d)	Ecological	Semi-natural woodland with oak, birch, alder ash and rowan. Several uncommon species occur in herb layer.
35. Three Castle Head V 72 26 40 ha	Heath	Ecological (B)	Heath communities are well-developed with large populations of the rock-rose, Tuberaria.
Local importance			
36. Argideen River & Courtmac-sherry Bay W 49 40 400 ha	Mudflats Saltmarsh	Ecological	The site has some importance as a wintering area for wildfowl. Well-developed saltmarsh in Flaxford inlet but cordgrass, Spartina anglica, is spreading elsewhere.
37. Aultagh Wood W 25 58 20 ha	Woodland(d)	Ecological	Mixed oak and birch wood.
38. Barley lake V 88 57 150 ha	-	Geomorphological	A good example of a glacial corrie.
39. Butlerstown lake W 92 73 21 ha	Lake	Ecological	Small lake surrounded by reedbeds and marginal bog.
40. Calf Islands V 95 26 90 ha	Heath	Ecological (B)	A site for the rock-rose, Tuberaria guttata, which occurs only in a few other locations in Ireland.
41. Cape Clear Island V 96 22 15 ha	Heath Marsh	Ecological	Well-documented site with small seabird colony and interesting flora in boggy areas. Bird observatory records bird migration and has built up valuable historical records.
42. Carrickshane Hill W 90 73 20 ha	Exposed rock	Ecological (B)	Limestone hill with species-rich flora, including the stonecrop, Sedum dasyphyllum.
43. Carrigacrump caves W 903 653 0.4 km section	-		Water-floored canyon passages occur in most of the eight cave entrances that lead out of the quarry.
44. Crookhaven V 78 24 18 ha	Heath	Ecological (B)	A rich heath flora occurs here on rocky ground with species such as the birds-foot, Ornithopus.

Name of Area	Haitat	Interest	Description
CORK			
Local importance			
45. Douglas River W 71 69 250 ha	Mudflats	Ecological (O)	A feeding and roosting area for shorebirds in Cork Harbour.
46. Dunderrow wood W 57 52 12 ha	Woodland (d)	Ecological	A wood on the west side of the Bandon estuary containing a high proportion of native species outside coniferous areas.
47. Durrus V 84 40 20 ha	Blanket bog	Ecological	A small area of bogland with a central pond; the surrounding area supports alder with oak and birch to west.
48. Eyeries Island V 635 512 200 ha	Exposed rock	Ecological (O)	A rocky island, nesting site for common and arctic terns; the latter fairly rare in Cork.
49. Gearagh reservoir W 33 70 765 ha	Wooldland (d)	Ecological	Mixed swamp forest (162 ha) with species-rich ground layer. Interesting and well-documented dragonfly fauna. Remnants of a formerly large and unique alluvial forest submerged by reservoir construction. The adjacent lake (603 ha) is sometimes important for dabbling duck and can hold 2,000 birds.
50. Kilkeran lake & Castlefreke dunes W 34 32 500 ha	Fen Lake	Ecological	Wetland showing vegetation transition from reed to willow communities. A locally important area in west Cork for wintering wildfowl.
51. Knockomagh wood W 091 289 9 ha	Woodland (d)	Ecological	Typical mixed oak and birch wood with some introduced species.
52. Lough Aderry W 94 74 22 ha	Lake	Ecological (O)	A small roadside lake with some reedswamp. It is a wintering area for wildfowl with small numbers of gadwall regularly present.
53. Lough Ailua W 20 66 370 ha	Lake	Ecological (O)	Lake surrounded by reedbeds and bog. Wintering area for duck and swans and breeding site for teal and mallard.
54. Lough Beg W 79 63 93 ha	Mudflats	Ecological (O)	Wintering area for wildfowl and waders, attracting roosting birds from a large part of Cork Harbour. Particularly important for waders e.g. golden plover.
55. Lough Namaddra & Lough West V 950 603 1 ha	Lake	Ecological (Z)	Mountain lakes at 410m. One of the only sites for the pea mussel, _Pisidium hibernicum_.
56. Oven's Cave W 551 697 0.5 km section	-	Geological	An easily-entered cave with fine scalloping on the walls and other features.
57. Roancarrig Beg V 788 464 4 ha	Exposed rock	Ecological (O)	A nesting site for terns.

Name of Area	Habitat	Interest	Description
CORK			
Local importance			
58. Rostellan Lough W 87 66 52 ha	Lake(s)	Ecological (O)	Inlet of Cork Harbour, now isolated from tidal influence. Open water at west end and some alder scrub at east end. Wintering wildfowl include pochard, tufted duck and snipe. Large numbers of little grebes, some of which breed here.
59. Sherkin Island W 02 25 100 ha	Heath	Ecological (B)	Diversity of plant communities with well-developed rocky heath. Species include the birds-foot trefoil, *Lotus subuliflorus*. The island has educational value and has an ecological study centre.
60. Shippool wood W 57 55 16 ha	Woodland (d)	Ecological	Some parts are semi-natural in character and have an ecologically interesting flora and fauna.
61. Sullane Bridge W 26 73 12 ha	Woodland(d)	Ecological	A mixed oak and birch wood occurs on the side of the river valley below the bridge. It has some ecological interest in view of the absence of such woods over a great part of the county.

Name of Area	Habitat	Interest	Description

DONEGAL

International importance

1. Aranmore island
B 06 01
7 km section

Exposed rock

Ecological (B)

The coastal cliffs are the site of a rare saxifrage, Saxifraga hartii, which is a form endemic to Ireland, resembling S. rosacea.

2. Lough Barra bog
B 92 10
700 ha

Blanket bog

Ecological

Western blanket bogs with many features of ecological interest despite marginal cutting. The area extends across the Gweebarra River to Lough Nanuroge. With present knowledge it is thought to be the best area of blanket peat in Donegal.

3. Glenveagh woods
C 01 19
94 ha

Woodland (d)

Ecological

Old natural woodlands, in places overgrazed by deer and showing poor regeneration. Dominated by oak and holly with a good variety of other species e.g. birch, rowan yew, juniper, whitebeam and bird cherry. Excellent development of lower plant communities characteristic of western oak-woods. The wood is responding to management and its value will gradually increase.

4. Horn Head
C 00 04
8 km section

Exposed rock

Ecological (O)
Geological

Inaccessible quartzite cliffs with interesting structural features especially at Micky's Hole where a horizontal slide is associated with inverted strata. The cliffs hold very large seabird colonies including the largest colony of razorbills in Ireland and Britain (45,000 prs). Guillemot (10,000 prs), puffin (250 prs), kittiwake (5,000 prs) and fulmar (2,500 prs) are also numerous.

5. Inch Lough
C 34 22
320 ha

Lake (s)

Ecological (O)

Shallow brackish lough surrounded by damp re-claimed fields. A productive site providing abundant food for several species of breeding duck and large numbers of wintering wildfowl. Landfall for migratory whooper swans with 1,500 once present in October. In winter these swans (700) are present with mute swan (250), pochard (600), wigeon (600) and coot (850). The most important wildfowl wetland in the county.

6. Malin Head
C 03 05
1.5 km section

Exposed rock
Shingle

Ecological (B)
Geomorphological
Geological

The highest, oldest and best preserved of the late glacial marine strandlines known in Ireland, the area is of great interest to Quaternary geologists. The coastal flora is also of interest here with oyster plant, Mertensia, and other species present.

7. Mullagh Derg
B 755 205
0.1 ha

-

Geological

A rare European occurrence of orbicular granodiorite, an igneous rock with differential sorting of minerals.

8. Slieve League
G 05 07
1,800 ha

Blanket bog
Exposed rock
Heath

Ecological (B)
Geomorphological

Quartzite cliffs capped by basal Carboniferous sandstones and conglomerates, they are an excellent example of marine erosion and are the highest in Ireland. Along the summit wet heath is particularly well-developed and it grades northwards into largely intact blanket bog. The backwall of the Lough Agh corrie supports the richest arctic-alpine communities in the county.

Name of Area	Habitat	Interest	Description
DONEGAL			
National importance			
9. Ardnamona wood G 96 84 29 ha	Woodland (d)	Ecological (B)	Well-grown trees on relatively fertile soil by Lough Eske. Woodland dominated by oak, which is regenerating, ash, alder with some rowan, birch, holly, hazel, willow and rhododendron. Typical ground flora with some rare herbs.
10. Ballintra C 920 680 0.5 ha	Grassland	Ecological (B)	Exposed limestone with herb-rich communities. The most northerly outpost of the limestone flora including the rock-rose, _Helianthemum nummularium_, at its only Irish site.
11. Barnes Gap C 094 242 C 085 265 0.5 ha	-	Geological	Two sites occur here, the first being an out-crop showing sheets of granite within a contact metamorphic zone. It is an important historical site. The other is a railway cutting exposing large skarn mineral deposits, rich in wollastonite.
12. Birra Lough G 87 69 390 ha	Lake(s)	Ecological	Shallow lake, enriched by shell sand, with extensive marginal reed beds. Important as a wintering area for whooper swan (300) and some pochard (260); also as a breeding area for some wildfowl. The third most important wild-fowl wetland in the county.
13. Bulbin mountain C 35 42 200 ha	Exposed rock	Ecological	Base-rich rocks supporting interesting communities of higher and lower plants, especially bryophytes.
14. Dunragh Loughs H 00 07 1600 ha	Blanket bog	Ecological	Large, very remote area of blanket bog containing several acid lakes. A good representative of an area of northern blanket bog, largely intact but planted with conifers along some of the perimeter.
15. Kilkenny pebble dyke G 775 980 0.5 ha	-	Geological	An intrusive dyke exposed at the surface. The dyke consists of three-faced pebbles in a granophyric matrix.
16. Lough Nacung B 08 00 200 ha	Blanket bog	Ecological (B)	The rare heather, _Erica mackaiana_, grows on the peat around the lake margin. One of the only three known sites for this Lusitanian species in Ireland.
17. Lough Nagreany dunes C 13 41 30 ha	Grassland Heath	Ecological	Undisturbed dune area with unusual heath vegetation of juniper, _Juniperus communis_, and willow, _Salix repens_, on higher areas.
18. Meenagoppoge bog B 96 22 100 ha	Blanket bog	Ecological	A fine example of a very wet, virtually intact blanket bog with numerous pools and a varied vegetation, dominated by deer-sedge, _Scirpus cespitosus_, in the eastern parts and bog rush, _Schoenus_, in the more central area.

Name of Area	Habitat	Interest	Description
DONEGAL			
National importance			
19. Owenbeagh bog C OO 18 17 ha	Blanket bog	Ecological	Intact blanket bog with an ombrogenous dome developed in the Glenveagh valley. Of considerable ecological interest, at the northern limit of the Irish blanket bog zone. One of the most interesting peatlands in the county.
20. River Foyle C 35 10 150 ha	Grassland Mudflats	Ecological	Roosting and feeding area for large numbers of swans and other wildfowl including internationally important flock of white-fronted geese (210) and whooper swans (350). Grey-lag geese (300) also occur, sometimes with 2,500 dabbling duck, especially mallard and teal.
Regional importance			
21. Ballyar Wood C 18 20 23 ha	Woodland(d)	Ecological	The best grown oakwood in the county with a canopy of oak and occasional birch and rowan. Hazel, blackthorn and holly form a well developed understorey - apparently regenerating Typical ground flora.
22. Ballyshannon G 900 610 0.5 ha	-	Geological	Exposure of Ballyshannon limestone lying unconformably on metamorphic rocks. A colonial coral, Syringopora, occurs 1 m above the unconformity. This section contrasts markedly with the north side of Donegal Bay where the transition is complete with sandstones below the limestone.
23. Blanket Nook C 30 19 67 ha	Lake(s)	Ecological (B,O)	Shallow, brackish lake with marginal marshy pools and wet pasture. A reed-swamp of club rushes, Scirpus maritimus, and S. tabernaemontani, fringes the western side of the lough. Important part of the Lough Swilly wildfowl area used for breeding and wintering. Whooper swans (550) present in November which move between Blanket Nook, Inch Lough and Port Lough. Also supports several uncommon plants.
24. Brockagh B 836 105 1 ha	-	Geological	Part of the Donegal granite contact zone showing intrusive relationships and a wide variety of rock types incorporated as xenoliths.
25. Bundoran foreshore G 80 58 4 km section	-	Geological	Limestone cliffs and intertidal rocks which are richly fossiliferous.
26. Carndonagh wood C 45 45 13 ha	Woodland(d)	Ecological	Old oakwood modified by man in the past. Oak, some birch and occasional rowan form the canopy. Hazel, willow and holly are included in the understorey.
27. Carradoan C 28 30 200 ha	Woodland(d)	Ecological	Old oakwood with birch, holly, hazel, hawthorn and blackthorn. Alder and willow in wetter areas. Variety of stages in succession from open pasture, through birch scrub to oakwood. The Back Wood is the most important area within the woodland complex.

Name of Area	Habitat	Interest	Description

DONEGAL

Regional importance

Name of Area	Habitat	Interest	Description
28. Creeslough wood C 06 30 19 ha	Woodland (d)	Ecological	Dominated by birch, with a variety of other deciduous trees, including beech east of Duntally Bridge. A rich birdlife is present.
29. Dunfanaghy C 00 36 400 ha	Lake(s) Grassland	Ecological (B,O) Geological Geomorphological	The lake and surrounding land are used by wintering wildfowl including white-fronted geese (30). The area is also important for some breeding duck. Extensive sand dune system with large dune slack with a variety of interesting plants and communities.
C 012 375 - C 025 377 1.5 km section	-		On the foreshore there is a good exposure of structural features associated with a slide.
30. Dunlewy B 932 191 0.1 ha	-	Geological	A granite contact zone, with rafts of granodiorite, occurs with a disused marble quarry. This has well-developed metamorphic minerals and deformational features.
31. Fahan Woods C 33 27 30 ha	Woodland (d)	Ecological	An oak/hazel woodland in very good condition with insect species of interest.
32. Finner dunes G 84 61 350 ha	Sand dunes	Ecological	Actively developing dune system, particularly in the Tullan strand area, illustrating plant successions typical of this sort of habitat.
33. Gartan Lough & Lough Akibbon C 00 01 450 ha	Lake	Ecological (B)	Fine examples of large oligotrophic lakes. Bird cherry, Prunus padus, and globe flower, Trollius, occur around the lake margins with interesting wet woodlands and scrub.
34. Gannivegil Bog B 82 06 450 ha	Blanket bog	Ecological	A well-developed area of blanket bog which has been partially cut. Water systems and their influence on the vegetation are of particular interest here.
35. Inishtrahull C 48 65 42 ha	Exposed rock	Ecological (O) Geological	Island formed of Lewisian gneiss, the most ancient rock found in Ireland, occuring also in Mayo and Galway. An important eider duck breeding colony.
36. Kildoney Point G 82 64 4 km section	-	Geological	Interesting and clearly visible deltaic sedimentary structures in Upper Calp sandstones.
37. Lackagh River C 09 31 1 km section	-	Geological	An interesting contact zone where the local granite meets ancient (Dalradian) quartzites.
38. Lough Derg H 00 07 900 ha	Lake	Ecological (Z)	Large, acid, mountain lake with a race of char and large colonies of breeding lesser black-backed and herring gulls.
39. Lough Eske G 09 08 750 ha	Lake	Ecological (B,Z)	Exceptionally large stocks of char occur in this lake. Several rare plants grow around the margins. Waterwort, Elatine hexandra, is found on mud, the caraway, Carum verticillatum in wet meadows.

Name of Area	Habitat	Interest	Description

DONEGAL

Regional importance

Name of Area	Habitat	Interest	Description
40. Mulroy Bay C 13 38 37 ha	Grassland	Ecological (O)	The islands form an important breeding site of sandwich terns. The marine algae in the bay have also been studied.
41. Murvagh Lower G 89 73 350 ha	Grassland Sand dunes	Ecological	Broad sand spit with a diversity of habitats including dunes on the western side and low-lying grassland grading into saltmarsh on the east. Southern part planted with conifers.
42. Poisoned Glen B 94 16 550 ha	Blanket bog Exposed rock	Ecological (B) Geomorphological	A fine west-facing corrie with very steep high walls and a peat-covered floor. Probably the finest corrie in the county. Several western plant species of interest occur.
43. Port Lough C 34 15 9 ha	Lake	Ecological(O)	Large areas of reedswamp and other marsh vegetation surround this moderately rich lake. Important for nesting and roosting water birds in the Lough Swilly area.
44. The Pullans G 94 70 0.3 km section	-	Geomorphological	The Blackwater river east of Ballintra flows through a series of unroofed caves with some intact passages remaining.
45. Roaninish B 65 02 13 ha	Grassland(s)	Ecological(O)	Small flat island covered with lush maritime grassland. Important breeding ground for arctic tern, eider duck and storm petrel. Barnacle geese (70) overwinter on the island.
46. Sessiagh Lough C 04 36 25 ha	Lake	Ecological (Z)	An acid lake with little or no visible benthic vegetation or marginal reedswamp but exceptionally high biomass. Supports brown trout, char and a breeding colony of black-headed gulls.
47. St John's Point G 70 69 350 ha	Grassland	Ecological (B) Geological	Narrow limestone peninsula with richly fossiliferous coastal cliffs and rocks and an interesting calcicole flora. This includes bloody cranesbill, Geranium sanguineum and the stone bramble, Rubus saxatilis.
48. Tory Island (parts) B 08 04 56 ha	Exposed rock	Ecological (O)	High cliffs on the eastern side hold large colonies of breeding auks (1,550), kittiwake (360 prs), common gull (50 prs), fulmar (260 prs) and chough. A variety of water birds on the lough in the north-west, includes several uncommon species.
49. Tranarossan C 12 42 30 ha	Grassland	Ecological	Well-developed wet machair grassland on windblown sand behind beach.
50. Trawbreaga Bay C 44 59 1650 ha	Mudflats	Ecological (O)	Important for wintering wildfowl, principally brent(150) and barnacle (120) geese. Sand dunes at Lag are of ecological interest.
51. West of Ardara-Maas Road G 06-07 09 1500 ha	Lake Blanket bog Grassland	Ecological (B,O)	Numerous habitats of considerable ecological interest occur in this area. Plant communities of shallow water include the pipewort, Eriocaulon, and interesting birds also breed. Sheskinmore Lough has rich communities of plants and birds because of the calcareous influence of windblown sand. The large dunes nearby are actively eroding under natural agencies.

Name of Area	Habitat	Interest	Description

DONEGAL

Local importance

Name of Area	Habitat	Interest	Description
52. Ballyness Bay B 09 03 950 ha	Mudflats	Ecological (O) Geological	Wintering area for brent geese and other wildfowl. Dunes are of general ecological interest. A very fine recumbent fold is exposed in rocks to the south of the pier.
53. Derrylaggy woods C 08 28 20 ha	Woodland (d)	Ecological	Interesting scrub and woodland communities with oak and beech at the north-east end.
54. Dooagh Isle C 40 50 400 ha	Grassland Sand dunes	Ecological	A complete dune ecosystem occurs on the western side with representative communities of beach, dune grassland and dune slack. A varied flora and bird fauna are also present.
55. Dooey dunes B 76 01 150 ha	Grassland Sand dunes	Ecological	Extensive dune system grading into heath at the northern end. Modified grassland on landward side is of ecological interest.
56. Fahan C 335 268 0.1 km section	-	Geological	An unusually good exposure of an isoclinal fold in slates occurs in a railway cutting here.
57. Fox Hall C 09 10 15 ha	Woodland (d)	Ecological	Open wet woodland with oak and hazel. Rich variety of associated organisms.
58. Glen Alla C 24 27 20 ha	Woodland (m)	Ecological	Mature estate woodlands of oak and beech and a few conifers. An introduced spurge Euphorbia amygdaloides, has become established in parts of the wood.
59. Kindrum Lough C 18 42 78 ha	Lake	Ecological (Z)	A shallow, acid lake close to sea level with a partial fringe of reedswamp and the stumps of ancient forest trees visible in the water. A population of char occurs.
60. Kinney Lough C 20 44 65 ha	Lake Fen	Ecologial (B,O)	Shallow lagoonal lakes supporting an interesting flora and wintering bird population.
61. Inishbarnog G 640 962 5 ha	Grassland (s)	Ecological (O)	Low-lying grassy island supporting a large colony of breeding eider duck and a small tern colony.
62. Inishduff G 647 723 2 ha	Exposed rock Grassland (s)	Ecological (O)	Small rocky, grass-covered island with breeding shag (50 prs) and gulls (400 prs). Barnacle geese sometimes winter on the island.
63. Inishkeeragh B 68 12 19 ha	Grassland	Ecological (O)	Breeding site for terns.
64. Leenan Valley woods C 01 01 50 ha	Woodland (d)	Ecological	Several patches of mature oakwood and extensive areas of birch and birch/oak scrub, representing stages of development of oakwood on rough open land.
65. Letterkenny woods C 01 00-01 50 ha	Woodland (d)	Ecological	Old planted woodland of oak, with some conifers, e.g. at Rockhill. Natural woodlands dominated by birch with some oak, as illustrated by Doon Wood.

Name of Area	Habitat	Interest	Description
DONEGAL			
Local importance			
66. Lettermacaward woods G 79 99 30 ha	Woodland(d)	Ecological	These woods are poorly grown with a low canopy of oak, birch and hazel. The more interesting stands occur around Cleengort Hill and Gweebarra Bridge.
67. Lough Fad-East C 54 39 15 ha	Lake	Ecological (Z)	Barren, acid, mountain lake surrounded by bog, with a race of char.
68. Lough Fad-West C 39 42 46 ha	Lake	Ecological (Z)	A similar acid mountain lake with char on the other side of Inishowen.
69. Lough Fern C 18 23 220 ha	Lake	Ecological (O)	Extensive marshes around the lake are used by breeding wildfowl. The flora also has unusual features.
70. Lough Finn B 09 00 250 ha	Lake	Ecological (Z)	Contains a race of char.
71. Lough Shore B 650 170 5.5 ha	Lake	Ecological (Z)	A small acid lake which supports a stock of fast growing rainbow trout. It is the only lake with a reproducing population of this introduced fish.
72. Melmore Lough C 125 435 4 ha	Lake	Ecological	A lagoonal lake formed by shell sand holding back the drainage from acid rocks. Interesting ecological conditions.
73. Muckish C 00 28 20 ha	Exposed rock	Ecological (B) Geological	A large flat-topped quartzite mountain with sand of exceptional purity, useful for optical glass manufacture. A few arctic-alpine plant species also grow on rock outcrops, for example, mountain avens, _Dryas_.
74. Mucross Head-Fintragh Bay G 69 76 10 km section	–	Geological	A coastal cliff and intertidal exposure of the Carboniferous with a fairly complete succession from basal schists, through an unconformity, up to marine limestones and shales. A wide range of rock types and sedimentary structures typical of many different deposition environments are visible.
75. Mullaghderg Lough B 76 20 92 ha	Lake	Ecological (B)	Shallow acid lough fringed with reed beds. Characteristically western plant communities contain several species of interest, such as the naiad, _Najas flexilis_. At the north end shell sand allows some calcicole species to be present also.
76. Rathmullan wood C 27 27 46 ha	Woodland(d)	Ecological	Mature deciduous woodland, mainly of oak with some beech. Birch scrub around the upper margins of the wood.
77. Rosapenna Lough C 110 380 2 ha	Lake	Ecological	Shallow, extremely calcareous lake with rich vegetation including a variety of stoneworts, _Chara_ spp.

Name of Area	Habitat	Interest	Description

DONEGAL

Local importance

78. Slieve Snaght B 92 15 850 ha	Exposed rock	Ecological (B)	Blanket bog containing several high-level lakes. A number of artic-alpine plants have been recorded growing on crags and in gullies.
79. Tormore Island area G 55 90 56 ha	Exposed rock	Ecological (O)	Breeding colonies of seabirds on island and nearby mainland cliffs, including auks (200 prs), kittiwake (470 prs), some fulmars and a few gulls.
80. Tullagh Point C 35 50 3 ha	Shingle	Ecological (B)	A stabilized storm beach with interesting maritime vegetation on its landward side. It merges into a small area of blanket bog.

Plate 3:   Bull Island, Co. Dublin. The north-east and most natural
            end, showing a circular former island and two major dune
            ridges (1906 and 1936) to its left. In between them is
            the Alder marsh. The saltmarsh on the right is the high
            tide roost of most of the shorebirds which feed on the
            mudflats of Dublin Bay (Dublin 2).

Plate 4:   Saltmarsh pools on the Bull Island, Co. Dublin, with
            a scant covering of glasswort, <u>Salicornia</u>. The short
            turf is of thrift, <u>Armeria</u> and has a patch of cord
            grass, <u>Spartina townsendii</u>, growing in it (Dublin 2).

Name of Area	Habitat	Interest	Description

DUBLIN

International Importance

1. Ballybetagh Bog
   O 20 20
   9 ha

   Habitat: Fen

   Interest: Ecological (B) Geological

   Description: The best late glacial site in the country and one of major importance for the European chronology of the period. Macrofossils, both plant and animal, occur in abundance and include tree willows, giant deer and reindeer. The site is overlain by fen vegetation.

2. North Bull Island, Dublin Bay
   O 22 37
   650 ha

   Habitat: Grassland Mudflats Saltmarsh Sand dunes

   Interest: Ecological(B,O,Z) Geological Geomorphological

   Description: A sand spit formed since the building of the North Wall, which is continually evolving, especially at the tip. Dune grassland and freshwater alder marsh contain an interesting flora and fauna whose colonization and spread can in many cases be dated. Saltmarsh has several unusual features and provides a roosting site for all the shorebirds in Dublin Bay. Up to 25000 birds of 15 species give the area the highest density of birds in the country. Wintering brent geese (1,100) are of international importance; pintail (450), shoveler (350), shelduck (900), and wigeon (4,000) of national significance. A well-documented site unique in Europe for its proximity to the capital city.

3. Rush
   O 272 542
   1 km section

   Habitat: -

   Interest: Geological

   Description: A conglomerate turbidite sequence of Carboniferous age displayed in a coastal section. This is the only exposure of such rocks in Ireland. It is also the type locality for a goniatite species.

National importance

4. Dalkey Sound-Sandycove
   O 27 26
   96 ha

   Habitat: Exposed rock(s)

   Interest: Ecological

   Description: Rocky shore with a well-researched marine fauna, including several rare species. Now reduced by marine pollution.

5. Howth Head & Ireland's Eye
   O 28 38
   500 ha

   Habitat: Exposed rock Heath

   Interest: Ecological(B,O,Z) Geological

   Description: Cliff sections of Cambrian quartzites and siltstones, showing outstanding sedimentary structures. A wide variety of habitats occur with a diversity of plants and animals (some uncommon species). Heath communities are well-developed and widespread with autumn gorse, Ulex gallii and the heathers, Erica cinerea and Calluna. Aberrant monster forms consistently occur in colonies of the red ant, Myrmica sabrinodis. These are unknown elsewhere in western Europe. The cliffs support substantial numbers of breeding seabirds including guillemot (250 prs), razorbill (200 prs), and kittiwake (1,000 prs). Ireland's Eye has larger areas of maritime flora and also larger seabird numbers, especially of guillemot (650 prs) and fulmars (50 prs).

6. Lambay Island
   O 31 50
   200 ha

   Habitat: Exposed rock Heathland Grassland

   Interest: Ecological(B,O) Geological

   Description: Ordovician volcanic and sedimentary rocks, shown as a good section in the cliffs and partially covered by glacial drift. Variety of plant communities which contain several interesting and rare species. Important seabird populations breed on northern and eastern cliffs, including puffin (100 prs), razorbill (1,400 prs), guillemot (10,000), kittiwake(1,450 prs), fulmar (75 prs), cormorant (320 prs), shag 760 prs), and possibly small numbers of Manx shearwater. Greylag geese (150) winter on the farmland.

Name of Area	Habitat	Interest	Description

DUBLIN

<u>National importance</u>

7. Malahide Estuary (Regional) 0 22 47 800 ha	Lake (s) Mudflats	Ecological (0)	The estuary has varied deposits of sand, mud and shingle. There are small patches of saltmarsh around the margins while an extensive stand of cord grass occurs in the north-east part. An important area for wintering wildfowl (1200), with brent goose (200), wigeon (400), goldeneye (150), red-breasted merganser (100) and great crested grebe (60). Wader numbers total at 4400, including knot, dunlin and oystercatcher. The estuary is almost closed from the north side by the Island.
8. a) Malahide Island (National) 024 46 150 ha	Grassland Sand dunes	Ecological (B) Geomorphological	This is a dune system based on a shingle spit and probably the best-developed and most natural one in the county. The area supports a varied flora and invertebrate fauna especially in the few dune slacks. There is also some saltmarsh at the point. Several tern species nest on the beach.
9. Malahide - Portmarnock 0 24 44 13 ha		- Geological	Foreshore exposures showing the only continuous section through the fossiliferous Lower Carboniferous rocks in the Dublin Basin. It is the type locality for several species of fossil coral.
10. Shanganagh 0 26 24 4 km section		- Geological	A cliff exposure of Quaternary glacial sediments. Two till types are seen, one from the Irish Sea area and the other from the Midlands.
11. Skerries - Rush 0 26 56 8 km section		- Geological	Foreshore and cliff sections exposing a unique series through Lower Carboniferous rock. Spectacular sedimentary structures occur in them, especially at Loughshinny.

<u>Regional importance</u>

12. Clondalkin quarries 0 070 310 3 ha		- Geological	A quarry exposure of limestone of the Visean Lower Carboniferous group with various turbiditic features. Exotic pebbles, from the Wicklow granite are incorporated in it, showing that this rock was uncovered during the formation of the limestone.
13. Curkeen Hill quarry 0 255 585 0.5 ha		- Geological	An exposure of fossiliferous Carboniferous reef limestones, the type locality for some fossil corals.
14. Feltrim Hill 0 19 45 16 ha	Grassland	Ecological Geological	A large active quarry in a Carboniferous reef-knoll. Interesting plant communities are associated with the limestone.
15. Glenasmole 0 09 22 50 ha	Woodland (d)	Ecological (B) Geomorphological	One of the highest drift-filled valleys in the country with naturally developing hazel woodland on the east side which contains an interesting flora and fauna.

Plate 5: Lambay Island from Portrane, Co. Dublin, showing pastures used by grey-lag geese in the winter. One of the major seabird colonies in the Irish Sea occurs on the northern and eastern cliffs. The volcanic rocks of the island bear little relationship to the sedimentary rocks in the foreground (Dublin 6).

Plate 6: Close folding of the rocks at Loughshinny, Co. Dublin. In the left half of the photograph two folds are clearly seen, seaweed growth picking out the underwater parts of the outcrop (Dublin 10).

Name of Area	Habitat	Interest	Description

DUBLIN

Regional importance

16. Killiney Hill 0 26 25 42 ha	Grassland Shingle	Ecological (B) Geological Geomorphological	Interesting mineralisation has occurred at the junction of the intrusive Wicklow batholith with the metamorphic aureole. Some unusual plants and insects occur on the drift banks beside the railway and on the shore. The whole area is a good example of a glacially-eroded mountain.
17. Portmarnock sand dunes 0 25 41 78 ha	Grassland	Ecological	Formerly the richest dune system in the county with a well-developed flora. The area of semi-natural vegetation is now confined to a zone outside the golf course. The saltmarsh is overgrown with cord grass but it still retains some ecological interest. Several uncommon invertebrates have been recorded here.
18. Portrane 0 260 501 2.5 km section	Exposed rock(s)	Ecological Geological	A coastal section complicated by faulting and folding. Ordovician volcanic and sedimentary rocks, including the Portrane limestone, the type stratum for a number of fossils. Lower on the shore the littoral communities are well-developed.
19. Rogerstown Estuary 0 23 52 400 ha	Mudflats	Ecological (O)	Two estuarine habitats separated by the railway line. The plant species eel grass, <u>Zostera</u>, tassel weed, <u>Ruppia</u>, alga, <u>Enteromorpha</u>, and glasswort, <u>Salicornia</u>, with invertebrates, provide food for large numbers of wintering wildfowl and waders. The second most important estuary for wildfowl (3300) and waders (5700) in the county. The area is of international significance for brent geese (475), and pintail (250); other species present in large numbers are teal (714), wigeon (1,540), shelduck (391), ringed plover (140), and godwits (250). The feeding area is being reduced by a refuse tip.
20. Royal & Grand Canals 0 07 38 0 07 32 28 km section	River	Ecological	Both canals contain interesting communities including species which have spread from the Shannon Basin, e.g. the grass, <u>Glyceria maxima</u>, arrowhead, <u>Sagittaria</u>, and flowering rush, <u>Butomus</u>. Seepage areas along the banks support a variety of species, some of which are unusual in the region.
21. Scalp 0 21 20 15 ha (also in Wicklow)	-	Geomorphological	The best and most accessible glacial outwash channel in the Dublin area. It is now a dry valley with block scree on both sides, covered by heath and woodland vegetation.
22. St. Doolagh's Quarry 0 205 422 2 ha	-	Geological	A flooded limestone quarry with some interesting calcicole plants growing nearby. The site is a reef-knoll and is the type locality for a number of fossil animals.

Name of Area	Habitat	Interest	Development

DUBLIN

Local importance

23. Balrothery
    Lake
    0 19 61
    14 ha
    | Lake | Ecological (B) | A reservoir with a fairly diverse flora which supports a variety of waterbirds. Two rare plant species occur here.

24. Bog of the
    Ring
    0 18 60
    43 ha
    | Marsh | Ecological (B) | A low-lying area of impeded drainage, this is the only sizeable marsh in the Dublin area. The plant communities include small areas of reedswamp with bulrush, Typha latifolia and bur-reed, Sparganium sp. and extensive wet meadows. The flora has certain elements of interest and the area is used by various waders and wildfowl. Several uncommon insects are recorded here.

25. Booterstown
    marsh
    0 200 306
    4 ha
    | Marsh(s) Saltmarsh | Ecological | A good example of a transitional freshwater/brackish swamp and saltmarsh supporting several uncommon plant species and a variety of wintering wildfowl and waders. Only brackish marsh between Dublin and Greystones.

26. Dingle Glen
    0 212 222
    7 ha
    | Woodland(d) | Ecological | A small dry valley some distance below the Scalp and formed as another glacial spillway. The block scree is being recolonized by woodland with holly, blackthorn, willow, hawthorn, ash, hazel and oak. Typical heath vegetation (gorse,bracken) on the slopes above. Moderately rich ground flora beneath the trees. Good bird, mammal and insect populations.

27. Loughlinstown
    woods
    0 253 228
    7 ha
    | Woodland (d) | Ecological | Originally planted, the wood has now assumed a natural character in age structure and form following regeneration. Beech, sycamore, elm, ash, blackthorn and hazel with alder and willow in the valley bottom. Good habitat for nesting birds including blackcap, woodcock and long-tailed tit.

28. Lugmore Glen
    0 064 252
    4 ha
    | Woodland (d) | Ecological (B) | Narrow valley cut in glacial drift, now covered by hazel woodland with some blackthorn, elder,goat willow and ash. A characteristically rich ground flora occurs as well as several bird species of interest.

29. Luttrellstown
    woodlands
    0 05 36
    44 ha
    | Woodland (m) | Ecological (B) | Long-established estate woodland with some semi-natural areas. Larger trees include sycamore, elm, beech, oak, ash and larch. Typical ground flora with a number of rare species. Supports a diverse bird and mammal fauna.

30. Portrane
    saltmarsh
    0 25 52
    20 ha
    | Saltmarsh | Ecological | An unusual saltmarsh community dominated by purslane, Halimione, which is spreading at the expense of sea lavender, Limonium spp.

31. Rockabill
    Island
    0 321 626
    2.5 ha
    | Exposed rock | Ecological (O) | Breeding site for terns and small colony of kittiwake (20 prs), and black guillemot (5 prs).

Name of Area	Habitat	Interest	Description
DUBLIN			
Local Importance			
32. Rush sandhills 0 26 53 15 ha	Sand dunes	Ecological(B)	Sand dunes in poor condition but known at one time to be a station for several interesting plant species.
33. Saggart Slade & Crooksling Glen 0 03 24 23 ha	Woodland (d)	Ecological	River valley with steep sides covered by trees - mainly planted. Fine specimens of beech, elm, ash, oak and birch with a typical, natural ground flora. Vegetation becomes more natural higher up the valley in Crooksling Glen.
34. Shenick's Island 0 268 596 0.5 ha	-	Geological	An angular unconformity occurs between Ordovician volcanic rocks and Upper Palaeozoic sandstones.
35. St. Catherine's Wood 0 02 35 15 ha	Woodland (d)	Ecological	Similar to Luttrellstown Wood but with more natural vegetation. Diverse bird and mammal fauna.

Name of Area	Habitat	Interest	Description

GALWAY

International importance

1. Boleyneendorrish
   River
   M 525 059
   1 km section

   –

   Geological

   An interglacial lake sediment with rich fossil flora of exotic species underlying boulder clay. The exposure is unique in Ireland and is the type locality for the Gortian warm stage. Nearby is an excellent transition from the Old Red Sandstone to Lower Carboniferous shales.

2. Errisbeg &
   bogland
   north
   L 70 40
   7,000 ha

   Blanket bog
   Exposed rock
   Heath

   Ecological (B)
   Geological

   Errisbeg has a varied geology of igneous rocks including the rare orbicular gabbro. It bears a stunted heath vegetation and its cliff flora includes the fern _Asplenium septentrionale_ at its only site in Ireland. A fine example of lowland blanket bog extends northwards with patches of heath on the rocky outcrops. Numerous small lakes have an interesting aquatic flora with oak/holly woodland surviving on islands. It is one of the most important blanket bog areas in Ireland and is largely intact. Numerous heather species are found including Dorset heath, _Erica ciliaris_, _E. mackaiana_ and _E. erigena_. Craiggamore Lough on the northern edge of the area is well-known for these species

3. Inishmore
   L 85 08
   600 ha

   Exposed rock
   Grassland

   Ecological (B,O,Z)

   An area with perhaps the most extreme development of limestone pavement and the plant communities characteristic of the Burren. Many species of great interest occur, both plants and insects and a few of them are absent from the mainland. Breeding seabirds include fulmar (150 prs), shag (75 prs), guillemot (1,200) and razorbill (300).

4. Little Brosna
   River
   M 98 11
   100 ha
   (also in Offaly,
   N. Tipperary)

   Grassland

   Ecological (O)

   A small part of this major wildfowl wetland occurs in Galway, especially Big and Friar's Islands in the Shannon and the callows at Muckinish and Melick. For details see Offaly.

5. Mannin Bay
   L 60 47
   400 ha

   Grassland
   Sand dunes

   Ecological
   Geological

   The beach material here is composed of coral-like material from the seaweed _Lithothamnion_. It is of considerable geological interest being one of the few examples of temperate carbonate production. An unusual calcicole dune grassland covers small areas around the bay, bringing in plants which cannot grow elsewhere in Connemara.

6. Rahasane
   turlough
   M 48 20
   150 ha.

   Grassland

   Ecological (O,Z)

   The last remaining large turlough in the country though it is unusual in having a permanent river, the Dunkellin, flowing through it. A strip of marsh vegetation follows the channel, elsewhere the damp grassland extends out to low limestone outcrops, sometimes covered by blackthorn and hazel scrub, the habitat of some butterflies of interest. The area is one of the most important wildfowl wetlands in Ireland and is unique in Europe. Whooper (200) and Bewick's swan (290) and wigeon (5,000) occur in numbers of international importance while shoveler (300) is of national significance. 17,500 waders occur at times, mainly golden plover. This was the site of discovery of the fairy shrimp, _Tanymastix,_ rare in Ireland and unrecorded in Britain.

Plate 7:   An aerial view of Rahasane turlough, Co. Galway, showing
            the extreme flatness of the basin. Ash trees are prominent
            in the hazel scrub in the foreground. Rahasane is highly
            unusual in having a permanent river, the Dunkellin, flow-
            ing through it (Galway 6).

Plate 8:   Aquatic vegetation grows thinly in these highly acid
            lakes near Maam Cross, Co. Galway. The quartzite slopes
            of the Twelve Bens rise steeply in the background
            (Galway 20).

Name of Area	Habitat	Interest	Description

International importance

7. Shannon River Athlone-Banagher M 98 23 200 ha (also in Offaly, Roscommon & Westmeath)	Grassland	Ecological (O)	The Shannon callows are a wintering site and migration route of great importance to birds. The wildfowl population of this section of the river includes wigeon (3,000), mallard (600), teal (600), wild swan (300) and white-fronted goose (100). Black-tailed godwit (500) occurs in spring and many other waders (5,000) are also seen. About one-eighth of the area occurs in Galway.

National importance

8. Aillebrack L 59 44 300 ha	Grassland Sand dunes	Ecological (B,O)	An extensive low-lying area of sand dunes with dune slacks, calcicole grassland and an area of saltmarsh. A golf course covers some of the ground. Rich in plant species and also the breeding site of several birds. The flora contains many species associated with the Burren in Clare that grow here because of the calcium content of animal and plant remains.
9. Bencorragh L 985 580 2 ha	-	Geological	Excellent examples of early Ordovician pillow lavas occur in the summit area of this mountain. A valuable exposure also occurs at M 005 593 in the Finny valley.
10. Castledaly M 513 091 0.5 ha	-	Geological	An exposure of interglacial peat occurs in a stream bed here which may prove to be of equal importance to Boleyneendorrish when it has been fully investigated.
11. Claggan M 001 505 0.1 ha	-	Geological	Unusual igneous rocks are well exposed at this site, including large mineral crystals. The rock type is an andalusite/muscovite pegmatite.
12. Derryclare & L. Inagh L 84 50 400 ha	Woodland(d) Lake	Ecological (B,Z)	Old, semi-natural oakwood with rich communities of lichens and invertebrates, which have been partly investigated. The area is now a Nature Reserve. Lough Inagh contains char and has interesting island vegetation also.
13. Dogs Bay L 69 38 150 ha	Grassland	Ecological (B) Geomorphological	A fine example of a tombolo. Much of the surface is covered by a rich calcicole dune grassland with many interesting species normally associated with western limestones. They include the eyebright, _Euphrasia salisburgensis_ and squinancywort, _Asperula cynanchica_. The sand is formed of foraminiferan shells.
14. Garryland & Coole M 42 03	Woodland(d) Turlough	Ecological (B,Z)	Oak and ash woodland occur here on limestone with one of the few semi-natural stands of pedunculate oak, _Quercus robur_. Rich associated flora and fauna with several unusual species. Good transition to aquatic communities, with a complex of turloughs.
15. Hill of Doon M 03 50 14 ha	Woodland(d)	Ecological	Mixed woodland with some fine areas of oak canopy with holly understorey. Other trees include yew, Scots pine and ash (regenerating). Well-developed ground flora, especially of ferns, mosses and lichens. A diversity of birds and mammals occurs.
16. Inishbernagh L 759 660 9 ha	-	Geological	Classic examples of coarse deep-sea Ordovician sediments are exposed on this island at the mouth of Killary Harbour.

Name of Area	Habitat	Interest	Description

GALWAY

National importance

17. Inishmaan L 93 05 480 ha	Exposed rock Grassland Marsh(s)	Ecological (B,O,Z)	Good examples of limestone communities are present including grassland, heath and pavement with many interesting species. Coastal lagoon has a large tern colony.
18. Lough Corrib (southern half) M 30 28 8,500 ha	Lake Fen	Ecological (O)	Low limestone shores surround much of this lake with extensive and little known fens at the southern end. The lake is of major importance for wildfowl holding 10% of the north-western European population of pochard (22,000) in autumn; coot (11,600) and tufted duck (5,000) are also major species. Some sections of the shore are valuable for breeding wildfowl (e.g. Mount Ross inlet). Important area for trout. The islands support several interesting wood-lands.
19. Knockash Hill M 640 114 10 ha	-	Geological	A natural cliff showing knoll reef forms and inter-reef cherty limestone. The transitional rock types are seldom so well shown.
20. Maam Cross L 90 44 1,000 ha	Blanket bog Lake	Ecological (B)	An extensive area of lowland blanket bog with oligotrophic lakes is found to the west of Maam Cross. Two unusual plant species are characteristic, the hair grass <u>Deschampsia setacea</u> and the bog cotton <u>Eriophorum gracile</u>. It is a lowland breeding area of golden plover and feeding area for white-fronted geese.
21. Muckanaght L 77 54 50 ha	Exposed rock	Ecological (B)	This mountain supports interesting upland heath, with some arctic-alpine plants extending to the summit. It is formed of schistose rocks in contrast to the quartzite of the rest of the Twelve Bens.
22. Mweenish Island L 77 30 500 ha	Exposed rock(s) Shingle	Ecological	A diverse marine flora and fauna occurs, well-documented by research.
23. Owenduff L 810 596 1 ha	-	Geological	An exposure of fossiliferous Silurian strata occurs at the bridge. The rock type is a conglomerate.
24. Renvyle Lough L 67 63 30 ha	Lake	Ecological (B)	Site of a rare water plant, <u>Hydrilla verticillata</u>, unrecorded elsewhere in Ireland and extinct in Britain. The lake is oligotrophic.
25. Rossroe peninsula L 761 652 1 ha	-	Geological	Exposures of early Ordovician black shales occur here with graptolites characteristic of Pacific faunas and unknown elsewhere in Europe.
26. Silver Island area, Lough Derg M 84 02 31 ha	Lake Marsh Woodland(m) Grassland	Ecological (B,O)	Several wooded island, reed-fringed lake-shore and marshes occur in this area. Large numbers of wintering wildfowl (1,200) are found although some of the dabbling duck are maintained by management. Pochard (600) is an important feature in autumn. The marsh flora is of exceptional interest, some of it grazed by deer. It includes the fleabane, <u>Inula salicina</u>, occurring in Europe but not Britain. Shores largely afforested but much juniper exists and forms the eastern limit of the Burren flora. The red alga <u>Bangia atropurpurea</u> occurs here as elsewhere around the lake.

Name of Area	Habitat	Interest	Description

GALWAY

National importance

27. Suck River
M 84 32
1600 ha

   a) Ballyforan-
      Ballinasloe
      600 ha

   b) Ballinasloe-
      Shannonbridge
      800 ha

   (also in Roscommon)

	Habitat	Interest	Description
27. Suck River	Grassland	Ecological (O)	The flooded callows of the Suck are valuable feeding areas for wintering wildfowl. The northern section is one of the few inland haunts of the white-fronted goose (100). Other species include wigeon (5,400) and wild swans, both Bewicks (100) and whooper (100). The area is also important for lapwing and golden plover (7,000).

Below Ballinasloe the overall value declines slightly but the callows support additional wigeon (2,600) and wild swan (300). This part of the area may be used by the goose population when bog exploitation starts above the town. |

Regional importance

	Habitat	Interest	Description
28. Abbey Hill M 30 10 60 ha (also in Clare)	–	Geomorphological	A major scarp feature forming the north-eastern boundary to the Burren hills and, to many visitors, the gateway to the region.
29. Angliham & Menlough Quarries M 290 305 3 ha	Grassland	Ecological (B) Geological	Good exposures of Galway black marble. Plants of calcareous grassland occur, including orchids such as Coeloglossum, Listera and Dactylorhiza, and scattered juniper bushes.
30. Annaghdown M 28 39 92 ha	Woodland(d)	Ecological	Fine example of an ashwood on limestone with a great diversity of species. A good example of zonation from lakeshore to wood occurs with associated plant communities well-represented.
31. Ballin Lough M 70 04 200 ha	Blanket bog	Ecological	Fine example of blanket bog on Old Red Sandstone in the Slieve Aughty mountains which are elsewhere widely afforested.
32. Ballycuirke Lough M 23 31 250 ha	Lake	Ecological	The catchment area of this limestone lake is made up of acidic rocks and blanket bog. The algae and invertebrates along the feeding rivers and in the lake have been found to be of interest.
33. Ballygar M 78 54 150 ha	Raised bog	Ecological	Extensive area of raised bog with some marginal cutting and colonisation by pine. Good example of hummock-hollow formation, typical of this type of bog.
34. Ballyglunin M 47 41 0.1 ha	–	Geological	An extensive series of caves and stream ways occur under the Abbert River at Ballyglunin. They were first discovered during drainage work on the river.
35. Ballynahinch Lake L 76 48 - 80 48 310 ha	Lake Woodland(d)	Ecological (B,Z)	Typical western oak woodland with the characteristic calcifuge flora. It is the type locality for the Irish whitebeam, Sorbus hibernica. Rich bird and mammal faunas. The lake is a lowland acid type and holds char.

Name of Area	Habitat	Interest	Description

GALWAY

Regional importance

36. Caherglassaun Lough
M 42 06
55 ha
Turlough — Ecological Geomorphological — A good example of a turlough where the zonation of plants is regulated by fluctuations of water levels. Flora is diverse and includes the yellow cress, _Rorippa islandica_.

37. Carna
L 79 31
3 ha
Heath — Ecological (B) — Between Carna and L. Sheedagh, wet heath occurs close to the road. On this the Lusitanian heather, _Erica mackaiana_, has one of its three Irish populations.

38. Cleggan Head
L 545 575
0.5 ha
– — Geological — The best Connemara exposures of Dalradian boulder beds with a glacial origin occur here.

39. Clifden
L 842 486
0.5 km section
– — Geological — A good exposure of quartzite occurs here with structural features of interest, such as rodding.

40. Cloonascragh bog
M 874 261
5 ha
Fen — Ecological (Z) — A fen developed between an esker and raised bog. One of the main sites for the snail, _Vertigo geyeri_, which is a declining species.

41. Cloonloughlin & Mount Talbot callows
M 82 53
70 ha
(also in Roscommon)
Grassland — Ecological (O) — The callows of the Suck on the Galway side form part of a wetland complex that includes a turlough in Roscommon. Wigeon (1,300), teal (680), shoveler (100) and pintail (75) occur in winter with waders such as lapwing (1,000) golden plover (2,000), dunlin (300). Black-tailed godwit (800) are regular on their Icelandic migration.

42. Cloughbally-more
M 40 11
150 ha
Woodland(d) — Ecological — A good example of an oak-ash woodland with a diversity of species and habitats, including limestone pavement.

43. Cregduff Lough
L 72 39
100 ha
Lake — Ecological (B) — A lowland acid lake with interesting communities of aquatic plants. Heath is well-developed on the granite outcrops nearby.

44. Doughruagh Mountain
L 76 60
11 ha
Lake
Exposed rock — Ecological (B,Z) — Five small bog lakes occur at 530m and contain several species of insects characteristic of arctic-alpine areas. Slopes of botanical interest with the fern, _Cryptogramma crispa_, and moss, _Herberta aduncta_, particularly abundant.

45. Finny River
M 000 592
2 ha
– — Geological — Very fine jasper is developed beside the Ordovician volcanic rocks in this area. It occurs in a wide variety of colours (see also Bencorragh above).

46. Gentian Hill & Lough Ruisin
M 25 22
130 ha
Grassland
Mudflats
Woodland(d) — Ecological (B,O) — The area contains several habitats of interest and of value in education. Lough Ruisin is a largely tidal bay, used in winter for feeding by wildfowl and waders, and in the autumn by roosting terns. Close to its entrance the drumlin of Gentian Hill occurs and its calcareous soils support a species-rich grassland, an outlier of the Burren flora with many of the same plants. At Silver Strand a beech stand planted on granite shows good woodland development and has an interesting fungal flora.

Name of Area	Habitat	Interest	Description

GALWAY

Regional importance

47. Glendollagh Lough
L 84 75
60 ha
| Lake Woodland(d) | Ecological (Z) | An acid lake of ecological interest because it contains char. Extensive oak woodland occurs near the shore with similar flora to Derry-clare wood. |

48. Gortnan Darragh
M 19 40
450 ha
| Exposed rock Grassland | Ecological (B) Geological Geomorphological | Extensive area of gently dipping limestone pavement with hummocky blocky ground to the east and south. The calcareous flora is well-developed and of great interest. It includes the moor grass, Sesleria, with more noticeable plants such as bloody cranesbill, Geranium sanguineum and mountain avens, Dryas. |

49. High Island
L 51 58
33 ha
| Grassland(s) | Ecological (O) | Site for breeding seabirds (Manx shearwater and storm petrel) and wintering barnacle geese (20). |

50. Knocknacoura
M 135 435
2 ha
| - | Geological | A section through the lower part of the Carboniferous limestone containing silicified coral faunas. |

51. Lissoughter
L 855 488
0.5 ha
| - | Geological | A fine exposure of Connemara green marble occurs here in a disused quarry. |

52. Lough Cutra
R 47 98
1,650 ha
| Grassland Woodland(d) | Ecological (B) | A limestone lake near Gort with the acid Slieve Aughty hills rising nearby. A diversity of habitats occurs with a mixed calcicole and calcifuge flora, including the Irish spurge, Euphorbia hyberna. |

53. Lough Rea
M 61 16
260 ha
| Lake | Ecological (O) | A highly productive limestone lake. Wintering wildfowl include mallard (240), pochard (210), coot (2,350) and shoveler (600). |

54. Merlin Park
M 340 260
1 ha
| - | Geological | A quarry exposure of Galway black marble in the Upper Visean limestone. Brachiopod fossils have been recorded. Maidenhair fern, Adiantum, grows here in abundance. |

55. Owenriff Falls
M 113 425
0.5 ha
| - | Geological | Faulted unconformity of basal Carboniferous granite breccia and sandstone overlying ancient rocks. |

56. Rushveala quarry
M 135 417
0.01 ha
| - | Geological | Good exposures occur here through the lower part of the Carboniferous. |

57. Shannagurraun
M 13 24
38 ha
| Woodland(d) | Ecological | Situated in the Owenboliska valley, this well-developed oakwood has an understorey of hazel, holly and birch. Rich flora of ferns, mosses and lichens. |

58. Streamstown Bay
L 580 555
1 km section
| - | Geological | A foreshore exposure showing Dalradian schists with fold structures intruded by granite. |

Name of Area	Habitat	Interest	Description

Local importance

Name of Area	Habitat	Interest	Description
59. Ballyconneely Marsh L 62 44 54 ha	Marsh(s)	Ecological (B,O)	Site for small numbers of wintering wildfowl and waders. The brackish marsh also has some botanical interest.
60. Blindwell M 350 590 10 ha	Turlough	Ecological (O)	Wetland used by small numbers of wintering and breeding wildfowl.
61. Bunowen L 595 430 10 ha	Exposed rock Marsh	Ecological (B)	Area of general ecological interest with alternating ridges of rock and lakes. Both habitats have an interesting flora.
62. Callow Lough M 72 34 60 ha	Lake	Ecological (O)	This wetland north-west of Kilconnell provides feeding for small numbers of wintering wildfowl and is a breeding area for some waders. The lake fluctuates in level and in some ways resembles a turlough.
63. Creganna marsh M 38 22 18 ha	Grassland	Ecological (O)	Feeding and roosting site for the Rahasane flock of white-fronted geese.
64. Dernasliggaun Wood L 82 62 19 ha	Woodland(d)	Ecological	The woodland is divided into western and eastern sections by the river Bunowen. Oak is dominant. Rich moss and lichen flora with characteristic western species, such as the filmy fern, Hymenophyllum tunbrigense and St. Patrick's cabbage, Saxifraga spathularis Danger of rhododendron spreading in wood.
65. Derryneen Lough L 890 460 9 ha	Lake	Ecological (Z)	Lowland acid lake of general ecological interest containing a race of char.
66. Drimcong M 21 34 37 ha	Woodland(m)	Ecological	Mixed deciduous/coniferous woodland on limestone with a good variety of species and habitats.
67. Furbogh M 19 23 48 ha	Woodland(d)	Ecological	Oak woodland with hazel/birch understorey and rich community of lichens, ferns and mosses. A rare lichen has been recorded here.
68. Glenicmurrin Lough M 00 31 150 ha	Lake	Ecological (Z)	Acid lake of general ecological interest containing a race of char.
69. Inisheer L 98 01 480 ha	Exposed rock	Ecological (B)	Interesting limestone communities with many of the Aran species present. Plants include the stonecrop, Sedum anglicum, normally a plant of acidic habitats.
70. Killaclogher M 55 40 750 ha	Raised bog	Ecological	An extensive raised bog, disturbed at edges, with typical flora.
71. Kinvarra rising M 37 10 0.1 ha	-	Geomorphological	The reappearance of the partially underground Gort river occurs on the foreshore here between high and low watermarks.

Name of Area	Habitat	Interest	Description
GALWAY			
Local importance			
72. Kylemore Lough L 77 59 150 ha	Lake	Ecological (B,Z)	This acidic lake has a fish fauna that includes char and an interesting aquatic and marsh flora with the quillwort, _Pilularia_.
73. Levally Lough M 53 54 67 ha	Turlough	Ecological	This large turlough is used by small numbers of wintering wildfowl and some breeding birds also.
74. Lough Aunemlagh L 70 50 13 ha	Lake	Ecological(Z)	An acid lake of interest since it contains both char and brown trout.
75. Lough Fingall M 42 18 300 ha	Grassland	Ecological	The lakeshore and esker support a good representation of Burren flora. Hazel scrub is plentiful.
76. Lough Hacket M 31 49 82 ha	Lake	Ecological	A limestone lake supporting small numbers of wildfowl and waders.
77. Lough Shindilla L 96 46 1,100 ha	Lake Woodland(d)	Ecological (B,Z)	Lake of general ecological importance containing char. Unusual aquatic vegetation is found along the lake margin and naturally developing woodland on island.
78. Marblehill M 710 050 0.5 ha	-	Geological	Quarry exposure of the Lower Carboniferous which shows the base of the massive reef limestones.
79. Newton Hill M 190 345 3 ha	Woodland(d)	Ecological	Birch and hazel are dominant species with occasional oak and hawthorn. A rich moss and lichen flora occurs.
80. Owenglin River L 750 510 0.5 ha	-	Geological	A fine exposure of Connemara green marble.
81. Rinville M 345 225 0.5 ha	-	Geological	A quarry exposure of Lower Carboniferous reef limestone.
82. Ross Lake wood M 19 37 150 ha	Woodland(d)	Ecological	Mixed woodland on limestone of general ecological interest with a diversity of habitats.
83. Tawin peninsula M 310 190 350 ha	Exposed rock(s) Mudflats	Ecological (O,Z)	The lagoon area is important for wintering wildfowl. Grey seal haul-out on boulder beach near lagoon entrance.
84. Tiaquin M 57 35 150 ha	Raised bog	Ecological	Fine example of a raised bog bordered by birch wood.

Name of Area	Habitat	Interest	Description

KERRY

International Importance

1. Akeragh Lough
A 76 27
250 ha

Lake(s)
Marsh

Ecological(O)

Shallow, brackish lagoon formed behind a line of high dunes. Black organic mud occurs beneath superficial shell and sand deposits. A highly productive habitat particularly at southern end. The fresh and saltwater plant communities show an interesting transition. Large numbers of wintering wildfowl are normally present, teal(3,500) and gadwall (150) in numbers of international significance. The regular important waders are lapwing (10,000) and curlew (4,000), but a very great variety of species occur in lesser numbers. It attracts many vagrant species, especially from North America, and occasionally is used for nesting by others.

2. Ballybunnion
Q 865 415
6 km section

—

Geological
Geomorphological

A good section through the Lower Carboniferous limestone and Namurian shales, richly fossiliferous. The site is also most important in Quarternary studies, showing the only interglacial raised beach cut into till in Ireland. A fine raised beach continues to the south around the Cashen estuary.

3. Ballyheigue
Q 347 298
0.1 ha

—

Geological

This is a locality containing fossils of the earliest gymnosperm plant assemblage in the Devonian.

4. Derrymore Island and Tralee Bay
V 74 11
950 ha

Mudflats
Saltmarsh
Shingle

Ecological(B,O)
Geomorphological

Mudflats, with cord-grass, _Spartina_, and eel grass, _Zostera_, support large numbers of winter wildfowl - brent geese(2,000), pintail (800) and wigeon (3,500) of international significance and waders. Saltmarsh flora to east of island with some uncommon species. Derrymore Island is a compound spit composed of a series of pebble beaches in a fine state of preservation. It is one of the best large pebble spits in Ireland.

5. Dunbeg
V 349 972
2 ha

—

Geological

An exposure where inverted bedding was first demonstrated by the use of sedimentary structures.

6. Gweestin valley
V 952 982
4 ha

—

Geological

Hard yellow Cretaceous chalk is exposed here in an outcrop in Barry's Glin, a glacial outwash channel. It is the only occurrence of such chalk outside Antrim.

7. Inch spit & mudflats
V 63 96
1250 ha

Grassland
Mudflats
Sand dunes
Saltmarsh

Ecological (O)
Geological (O)
Geomorphological

The spit holds the finest dune belt in the county with a representative west coast dune flora. The saltmarsh on the east grades into extensive mudflats with large areas of eel grass. Wintering area for large numbers of wildfowl and waders: of international significance for wigeon (6,800) in autumn, pintail (2,500) and shoveler (1,500) in winter and brent goose (4,000) in autumn. Large numbers of teal (2,300) also occur.

Plate 9:   Akeragh Lough, Co. Kerry, like most coastal marshes a
           lagoon formed by sand dunes blocking a stream outlet.
           The calcareous windblown sand and the shallow water give
           it a high productivity, much greater than the adjacent
           rushy fields (Kerry 1).

Plate 10: The spit of Derrymore Island, Co. Kerry, with a high
           western edge of shingle protecting the finer sediments
           of saltmarsh to the east. Note the pattern of accretion
           of shingle as a series of separate ridges (Kerry 4).

Name of Area	Habitat	Interest	Description
KERRY			
International Importance			
8. Inishtearaght V 18 94 27 ha	Exposed rock Grassland (s)	Ecological(O,Z)	A steep-sided island, covered in loose scree with an incomplete cover of vegetation. Supports large numbers of breeding seabirds including storm petrel (25,000 prs), puffin (7,500 prs) and kittiwake (400 prs). Several unusual races of insects have developed because of isolation.
9. Killarney Valley V 93 84 6500 ha	-	Ecological(B,O,Z) Geological	A large unit of exceptional ecological interest, the area is well-known for having the best development of oceanic woodland in the country, if not in Europe.
a) Derrycunnighy & Galway's Wood (International) V 89 80 136 ha	Woodland(d)	Ecological(B,Z)	The most natural oakwoods occur at the head of the valley, though they were much used for charcoal production at one time. This is oak/holly wood in its classic form with rich communities adapted to constant moisture. The ground flora of higher plants is limited but is made up for by the striking growth of ferns, mosses and lichens covering all available surfaces. They include many unusual species rare or unknown elsewhere in Ireland and some with sub-tropical affinities. Animal and bird life is similarly well-developed and is rich in insects and other invertebrates.
b) Muckross Woods (International) V 95 86 150 ha	Woodland(c,d)	Ecological(B)	This area consist of an eastern part on limestone which is yew wood (Reenadinna) and a western section of oaks on sandstone, offering a valuable contrast. The yew wood is the best and almost the only stand in the country. Some other trees are mixed in, either in marshy hollows where ash is common or on the lakeshore where the strawberry tree, aspen and whitebeam, <u>Sorbus anglica</u>, occur.
c) Tomies Wood (National) V 91 88 105 ha	Woodland(d)	Ecological(B,O) Geomorphological	This woodland is a comparatively open oakwood with some birch, consistently grazed by sika deer. The trees are up to 10 m high. The area is almost free from rhododendrom which causes problems in much of the valley. There is a good bryophyte flora, especially near streams and a rich bird fauna also. A fine lateral moraine occurs above the wood on the hillside.
d) Torc Waterfall (National) V 269 843 3 ha	Exposed rock	Ecological(B,Z)	The stream flora is best seen at Torc waterfall which lies in a narrow gorge with native and introduced tree species in it. A luxuriant growth of mosses, liverworts and ferns occurs on rock surfaces, tree bark and soil, and has very great interest. A number of rare invertebrates has also been found, including molluscs as well as insects.

Plate 11: Inishtearaght, with Great Blasket Island in the distance. One of the most important sites for breeding seabirds in Ireland, especially for storm petrels, puffins and kittiwakes (Kerry 8).

Plate 12: The Killarney valley, Co. Kerry, the site of the largest stands of semi-natural forest in the country. The tree-line on the left is kept low down by grazing animals but extends up the stream valleys on inaccessible ledges. Glaciated rocky knobs break through the blanket bog by the lakes (Kerry 9).

Name of Area	Habitat	Interest	Description

KERRY

International Importance

9. **e)** Killarney Lakes (National) V 90 81 V 96 85 V 95 89 600 ha — Lake Woodland(d) — Ecological(B,O,Z) Geomorphological — The Killarney lakes have a fauna with a northern element in it. It includes two interesting fish, a land-locked twaite shad, _Alosa fallax_, and a race of char, _Salvelinus_. Lough Leane supports relatively large numbers of wintering wildfowl, for example, tufted duck (850), pochard (870) and teal (300) and some breeding wildfowl and waders also. Many of the islands have an interesting vegetation which has been little subjected to grazing. Arbutus Island in the Upper Lake and Brown, Cow, and Lamb's Island in Lough Leane are particularly valuable. The limestone shores of Muckross Lake and Lough Leane have been eroded in places by the acid lake waters and have assumed unusual shapes.

f) Newfoundland Bog (Regional) V 92 82 44 ha — Blanket Bog — Ecological — A wet blanket bog occurs beside the Long Range with several unusual features. It is cut at intervals by rocky ridges with heath plants, including strawberry tree.

g) Ross Island (Regional) V 94 88 62 ha — Woodland(d) Fen — Ecological(B) Geological — Ross Island is similar to Reenadinna though yew is replaced by ash with some planted beech and large conifers. The base-rich soil supports a well-developed ground flora with interesting marsh and fen plants on the lake margin. Here maritime species also grow, some on the spoil heaps of the reworked Bronze Age mines that were used for copper and cobalt.

h) Lough Crincaum (National) V 932 823 1 ha — Lake — Ecological — A small acid mountain lake on Cromaglen mountain. It is the type locality for a snail, _Limnaea involuta_, unrecorded elsewhere.

i) Doogary Wood (Regional) V 90 84 20 ha — Woodland(d) — Ecological — An open birch/oak wood near the tree line. Development of the trees and ground vegetation has been stunted by prolonged grazing but it remains some of the highest woodland in the country.

10. Lambs Head V 53 57 100 ha — Heath — Ecological(B) — A rocky headland of Old Red Sandstone covered by acid heathland and shallow blanket bog. The Kerry lily, _Simethis planifolia_, grows here. It is a plant otherwise restricted to France, Spain and the Mediterranean.

11. Little Skellig V 270 620 8 ha — Exposed rock — Ecological(O) — Site of the third largest colony of gannets (20,000 prs) in the North Atlantic. Other nesting seabirds including kittiwake (1,120 prs), razorbills (40 prs), and guillemot (600).

Plate 13: Torc waterfall,

Plate 13

Torc Waterfall, Co. Kerry. The
high humidity in the gorge
favours mosses and ferns. The
species in the photograph
include the natural oak,
Quercus petraea and rowan and
the introduced sycamore. (Kerry 9).

Plate 14: Muckross Lake, Killarney, Co. Kerry, in winter showing
the oakwoods with their understorey of holly and occasionally the dark outlines of a strawberry tree, Arbutus.
In the foreground is a thin reedswamp of Phragmites
(Kerry 9).

Name of Area	Habitat	Interest	Description
KERRY			
National Importance			
12. Bay View & Oyster Hall Q 762 150 3 ha (1 km section)	−	Geological	This area includes a quarry exposure of a Lower Carboniferous reef and slumped striped limestones associated with it. On the foreshore a complex interglacial deposit occurs. It includes silts and peats overlain by a thick soliflucted sequence and is probably Gortian in age.
13. Brandon Mountain Q 46 11 4,000 ha	Blanket bog Exposed rock	Ecological(B,Z)	An extensive area of intact blanket bog with cliffs at higher levels. These have the greatest concentration of alpine and arctic-alpine plant species in Kerry. Rare species of invertebrates have also been taken on the mountain.
14. Caragh Lough V 71 88 115 ha	Lake Woodland (d)	Ecological(B) Geomorphological	A rich aquatic flora, both submerged and visible, occurs in the lake with many interesting invertebrates. Patches of oak woodland are found on the steep slopes at the south end of the lough. The valley to the north contains the best example outside the Alps of recessional moraines associated with a mountain glaciation. The outermost ring reaches Cromane.
15. Cloger Head & Cove Q 32 03 33 ha	−	Geological	Fine examples of Silurian volcanic rocks occur here with richly fossiliferous associated strata. Clogher Cove is the type site for one of the Silurian sedimentary formations.
16. Gap of Dunloe V 87 85 360 ha	−	Geomorphological	This spectacular landmark is the best example of a glacially-breached watershed in Ireland. There is a good sequence of lateral and recessional moraines at its mouth.
17. Great Skellig V 25 61 18 ha	Exposed rock	Ecological(O)	Important site of nesting seabirds, particularly puffin (6,500 prs), storm petrel (10,000 prs), Manx shearwater (5,000 prs) razorbill (600) and kittiwake (950 prs).
18. Inch-Anascaul 0 62 00 50 ha	Grassland	Ecological(Z) Geological	High coastal cliffs of glacial drift, partly vegetated. An interesting invertebrate fauna occurs. The foreshore here has two outcropping conglomerates and is the type site for one of them - the Inch conglomerate.
19. Kilmurry Bay V 59 99 1 km section	−	Geological	Large scale sand dunes are preserved in rocks of Devonian age on Acres Pt. It is probably the best example of these structures in Europe.

Plate 15: Active dune development at the southern end of Banna
Strand, Co. Kerry, with the Slieve Mish mountains behind.
Many erosional pockets can be seen with thick growth of
marram grass, Ammophila, on the landward side. (Kerry 1).

Plate 16: Cliff scenery in the Blasket Islands, Co. Kerry. The
slopes above the cliffs are the nesting grounds for
puffin and manx shearwater. Storm petrels prefer the
cavities in screes and cliffs, as on Inishtearaght.

Plate 17:   Part of the gannet colony on Little Skellig. The steeply
            dipping rocks offer many nesting sites and the birds
            often build close together, just outside pecking range.
            Adult gannets are completely white except for their black
            wing-tips (Kerry 11).

Name of Area	Habitat	Interest	Description
KERRY			
National Importance			
20. Lough Gill Q 58 13 350 ha	Lake Fen Sand dunes	Ecological(B,O,Z) Geomorphological	The Castlegregory spit is a large tombolo which has grown to link some of the Maharee Islands to the mainland. Lough Gill occurs in its centre and it is shallow and base rich with good feeding for fish and birds. Large numbers of wildfowl winter on the lake. At different times teal(4,000),shoveler(1,500) and tufted duck(2,000)have occurred with 100 gadwall. There is also a significant nesting population. The dune flora is probably the richest of its kind in the county. The natterjack toad has a flourishing colony in the area.
21. Mangerton V 97 80 1,500 ha	Blanket bog	Ecological(B,Z)	The western slopes of the mountain are covered by upland heath and form the main grazing area of the Kerry population of red deer. The summit blanket bog and the cliffs around the Horse's Glen and the Devil's Punchbowl have a concentration of arctic-alpine plant species. Higher plants, lichens and bryophytes are of interest.
22. Puffin Island V 34 73 51 ha	Exposed rock Grassland	Ecological(O)	Island situated relatively close to the mainland and important for nesting seabirds. Probably largest colony in Ireland of Manx shearwater (15,000 prs), with puffin (3,700 prs), fulmar (500 prs), storm petrel (1,000 prs), guillemot (175), razorbill (675 prs) and kittiwake (170 prs).
23. Rossbehy V 67 93 94 ha	Sand dunes Saltmarsh	Ecological(B,Z) Geological	A sand and shingle spit enclosing saltmarsh and mudflats on the eastern side. Interesting strandline flora with some unusual animal species also. Wintering wildfowl feed on the mudflats. In the cliff just to the west of the spit a well-exposed Quarternary sequence occurs. It shows a raised beach, two tills, and thick soliflucted deposits and is a type site.
24. Uragh Wood & Cloonee Loughs V 84 64 250 ha	Woodland(d) Lake	Ecological(B,Z)	The whole valley is a fine ecological unit with great diversity. Uragh wood is a rather uniform Atlantic oakwood on a shallow soil,fairly open with quite small trees. The main species are oak which is regenerating,with birch and rowan. A good variety of other woody species includes aspen, strawberry tree, and juniper. It has a relatively poor ground flora. The lake and associated marshy gound contains several plant species of interest and char also occur.
Regional Importance			
25. Ardagh Bog V 983 884 9 ha	Raised Bog	Ecological(Z)	The bog has developed by succession from a lake similar to the nearby Ardagh pond. Somewhat similar to a raised bog, except that it is partially wooded by birch. Surrounded by a ditch which supports more base-demanding species. Some rare aquatic invertebrates have been recorded here.

Name of Area	Habitat	Interest	Description
KERRY			
Regional Importance			
26. Ballaghisheen Bog V 68 80 300 ha	Blanket bog	Ecological	Intact blanket bog with fully representative plant communities.
27. Barrow Harbour Q 73 17 400 ha	Mudflats Exposed rock	Ecological(B,O)	The harbour is surrounded by limestone outcrops and ridges of glacial drift. Eel-grass, _Zostera,_ grows extensively on the mudflats. Important for wintering wildfowl - shoveler (350), teal (340), mallard (220) and wigeon (200) and a number of interesting plant species on the limestone.
28. Beginish Island V 41 78 10 ha	-	Geological	The best exposure of the Devonian volcanic rocks of the area occurs on this island beside Valentia.
29. Boughil & Lough Barfinney V 85 76 25 ha	Grassland Lake	Ecological(B,Z)	The rocky slope overlooking Lough Barfinney, consists of a series of small cliffs above a scree of large rocks. The cliffs are one of only three sites for alpine lady's mantle, _Alchemilla alpina_, in Ireland. The lake has been the site of an experiment in lake fertilization to study brown trout growth response.
30. Cashen River Estuary Q 89 36 27 ha	Mudflats	Ecological(B)	The tidal mud is colonised by a spike rush _Eleocharis parvula_ - a plant which has been found in only one other place in Ireland.
31. Coomasaharn Lake V 63 84 155 ha	Lake	Ecological(Z)	Elongated glacial lake surrounded by acid grassland, blanket bog and scrub. The lake contains a race of char which has not been taken in any other Irish lake.
32. Fahamore Q 60 19 2.5 km section	Exposed rock(s)	Ecological(B) Geological	Low limestone shore with a good example of a reef structure. It is formed of a series of inter-connecting pools which support rich marine communities including many southern species. The agar seaweeds _Gelidium_ and _Pterocladia_ are especially abundant.

Name of Area	Habitat	Interest	Description

KERRY

Regional Importance

Name of Area	Habitat	Interest	Description
33. Fermoyle Q 54 13 54 ha	Marsh(s)	Ecological	Fermoyle island is linked to the mainland by a sand isthmus and is itself largely covered by sand dunes, which are in an active state of change. The marsh is the main centre of ecological interest because it was formerly fresh but is now inundated with seawater. The communities are constantly changing.
34. Inishvickillane V 21 91 100 ha	Grassland (s)	Ecological(O,Z) Geological	Important island for nesting seabirds, particularly storm petrel (10,000 prs), and large numbers of Manx shearwater (1,000) Fulmar (170 prs), razorbill (165 prs), puffin (225 prs) and great black-backed gull (165 prs) also occur with small numbers of other species. Some interesting Lepidoptera are found here as on the other Blasket Islands. Excellent exposures of Silurian sedimentary and volcanic rocks can be seen.
35. Lehid Harbour V 78 63 32 ha	Woodland(m)	Ecological	A diversity of habitats supporting rich communities. Woodland contains mature oak with planted pine and fir and areas of birch. There is a diverse ground flora. It is an extremely sheltered marine habitat with terrestrial vegetation overhanging the sea.
36. Lixnaw Q 90 30 0.2 ha	-	Geological	A working quarry in striped Carboniferous limestone of Visean age. This is an unusual and distinctive rock type.
37. Lough Doon Q 50 06 98 ha	-	Geomorphological	One of the best-preserved and most complete examples of a corrie, striated lip and associated moraines. It is also easily accessible.
38. Lough Nagarriva V 969 606 2 ha	-	Ecological(Z)	High acid lake, the type locality for the pea mussel _Pisidium hibernicum_. The Nagarriva population represents a very aberrant form.
39. Lough Yganavan V 70 95 180 ha	Lake Marsh	Ecological(Z)	A low-lying lake with an interesting fauna which includes the natterjack toad.
40. Magharee Islands Q 58 22 29 ha	Exposed rock Grassland	Ecological(O) Geological	Low limestone islands showing many fine exposures of Carboniferous reefs. Important for wintering barnacle geese (300) and breeding seabirds, including storm petrel (150 prs), cormorant (60 prs) shag (130 prs), and common gull (80 prs) - a restricted species in the southwest. Arctic and common terns also breed.
41. Parkmore Point V 390 970 5 ha	Exposed rock(s)	Ecological	Small promontory close to Slea Head, open to the Atlantic swell. Irregular platforms of sandstone or conglomerate occur with well-developed floral and faunal zonations which can be correlated with slope and shelter.

Namd of Area	Habitat	Interest	Description
KERRY			
Regional Importance			
42. Puffin Sound-Horse Island Cliffs V 35 66 5 km section	Exposed rock	Ecological(O)	This is probably the most important breeding area for choughs in the country and they occur at high density. Flocks of up to 300 have been recorded.
43. Rossdohan Island V 72 64 23 ha	Woodland(m)	Ecological(Z)	Informal garden with natural regeneration of many introduced species including tree ferns. The area gives an impression of a southern hemisphere woodland with species from Australia, South America and South Africa. Rich insect fauna including a naturalised stick insect, Clitarchus hookeri, also occurs.
44. St. Finnan's Bay V 389 673 2 km section	-	Geological	A good coastal section with fossil fish localities that indicate the Iveragh Peninsula rocks are mainly Upper Devonian in age.
45. Slea Head V 33 96 11 ha	Grassland	Ecological(Z) Geological	Characteristic maritime cliff flora with an interesting insect community. The Dingle formation is well-exposed in the cliffs and rock outcrops.
Local Importance			
46. Ballylongford Bay Q 99 46 410 ha	Mudflats	Ecological(O)	A rich feeding area in the Shannon Estuary having up to 1,400 wildfowl(dabbling duck) and 2,100 waders.
47. Beal Point Q 90 48 33 ha	Sand dunes Saltmarsh	Ecological Geological	Sand dunes formed by several compressed dune ridges without dune slacks. Typical flora but ecologically important because of an absence of grazing. Salt marsh area near river mouth of interest for several species. Interesting Carboniferous rocks outcrop in the vicinity.
48. Beginish Island (Blaskets) V 28 98 15 ha	Grassland(s)	Ecological (O)	Breeding site for terns. Other breeding seabirds include storm petrel (100 prs), small numbers of black guillemot, shag and three gull species.
49. Camp valley Q 70 06 0.1 ha	-	Geological	A fine limestone glacial erratic is found in the stream valley here.
50. Carhoo West V 43 99 14 ha	Woodland(d)	Ecological	Originally planted with sycamore and beech but later colonised by alder, willow, oak and rhododendron. Two unusual liverworts have been recorded in the vicinity. Diverse bird life.
51. Carrigawaddra W 08 82 32 ha	Woodland(d)	Ecological	Cliff and block scree becoming colonised by a luxuriant forest vegetation. Flora similar to the Killarney woods but not subject to grazing.

Name of Area	Habitat	Interest	Description
KERRY			
Local Importance			
52. Church Hill Q 760 170 4 ha	Exposed rock	Ecological(B)	A small rocky limestone ridge in pastureland with several unusual plant species.
53. Cromane Point - Roscullen Point V 70 00 1,300 ha	Mudflats	Ecological(Z)	Large area of mudflats and saltmarsh free of cord-grass. The Cromane peninsula is of morainic origin while the Point is a spit. A locally important area for wintering wildfowl. The natterjack toad also occurs.
54. Derrynane V 51 58 37 ha	Marsh(s)	Ecological(B,Z)	Extensive area of salt marsh and inundated fields covered by vegetation with a range of coastal community types and a number of rare plants. A variety of shore birds use the area and the other fauna is also of interest.
55. Doohilla Quarry V 390 770 8 ha	Exposed rock	Ecological(O)	A disused slate quarry which supports an important colony of breeding choughs (20 - 30 prs).
56. Dooneen Wood R 016 125 9 ha	Woodland(d)	Ecological	Predominantly oak woodland situated on clayey soil on the southern escaprment of the Namurian shales. Other tree species include rowan, willow, hazel and ash. Diverse ground flora and a variety of animal species.
57. Glanleam Wood V 41 77 17 ha	Woodland(m)	Ecological(B)	Semi-natural wood composed of a mixture of native and sub-tropical species which have become naturalised. The area supports the finest collection of certain hybrid saxifrages (S. spathalaris x hirsuta in Ireland.
58. Glanmore Lake V 78 56 80 ha	Woodland(m)	Ecological	The lake is open to north and east but on steep slopes on the west side there is a planted woodland of silver fir and other species, with dense undergrowth of rhododendron. Important for nesting bird populations. Islands with fragments of natural woodland including strawberry tree, oak and holly.
59. Graigues Wood V 590 640 6 ha	Woodland(d)	Ecological	Vigorously regenerating oakwood, unusual in county, which is spreading onto surrounding areas of blanket bog. Main trees are oak, birch willow and holly. Poorly-developed ground flora, as yet.
60. Illaunabarnagh & Mucklaghmore Island Q 68 22 0.5 ha	Grassland	Ecological(O)	Small islands with colonies of breeding terns and cormorants(30 prs).

Name of Area	Habitat	Interest	Description
KERRY			
Local Importance			
61. Inishabro V 21 93 54 ha	Grassland (s) Exposed rock	Ecological(O)	Locally important site for a variety of breeding seabirds, in particular Manx shearwater (1,000 prs), storm petrel (475 prs), razorbill (525 prs), guillemot (150 prs) and puffin (500 prs); also kittiwake , shag and black-backed gull.
62. Inishtooskert Q 24 00 95 ha	Exposed rock	Ecological(O)	Locally important for breeding seabirds. particularly storm petrel (4,000 prs) and great black-backed gull (300 prs).
63. Kilgarvan Wood W 02 73 20 ha	Woodland(d)	Ecological	A relatively young wood on boulder clay. Mainly oak with some rowan and birch. Regeneration is good but not abundant. Moderately rich ground flora.
64. Lough Acoose V 77 85 69 ha	Lake	Ecological(Z)	Open upland lake surrounded by bog covered slopes with representative plant and animal communities. The blanket bog to one side has been flooded by a rise of water level. A race of char occurs in the lake.
65. Mucksna Wood V 900 990 6 ha	Woodland(m)	Ecological	Well-grown trees of native and introduced species including fir, pine, oak, beech, ash, sycamore, hazel and holly. One of the few woods in the county on fertile soil at near sea level. There is a well-developed ground flora, and a varied bird fauna.
66. Roughty River near Morley's Bridge W 04 75 10 ha	Exposed rock	Ecological(B)	Several unusual plant species grow on the exposed rocks cut by the river and a rare form of hawkweed has also been recorded. The adjacent blanket bog has a fully representative flora.
67. Spanish Island V 750 590 1 ha	Shingle	Ecological(O)	A small island close to the shore in Kilmakilloge Harbour. Breeding site for terns.
68. Tarbert Bay R 07 47 27 ha (also in Limerick)	Mudflats	Ecological(O)	An important site for wading birds(2,000) in winter, with some wildfowl (600).

Name of Area	Habitat	Interest	Description
KILDARE			
International Importance			
1. Pollardstown Fen N 78 17 150 ha	Fen	Ecological (B,Z)	This is the best developed fen in the country and it is reputed to have the largest area of saw sedge ,Cladium, in western Europe. The fen is relatively recent in origin and its present ecological interest is maintained by alkaline drainage water percolating from the Curragh gravels. Because of the rarity of the habitat, its animal communities are also of interest, especially the molluscs.
National Importance			
2. Carbury Bog N 68 63 320 ha	Raised bog	Ecological	A very well-developed raised bog with extensive hummock hollow regeneration and some wet pools. It appears to be the most intact of the bogs in the East Midlands and is relatively unaffected by drainage.
3. Chair of Kildare and Grange Hill N 72 18 100 ha	-	Geological	Inlier of Ordovician volcanic strata surrounded by reef limestone. The limestone reefs are also of Ordovician age and they contain a rich and well-documented tribolite fauna.
4. Curragh N 77 12 3500 ha	-	Geological	A unique deposit of fluvio-glacial gravels, in many places about 70 m in thickness. It is a source of water for many of the rivers and marshes nearby, including Pollardstown Fen.
5. Liffey valley N 93 - 84 10 2 km section	Woodland(d)	Geomorphological Ecological(B)	Broad floodplain with classical meander formations, some of the finest in Ireland. Patches of ash woodland surrounded by dense growth of sedges, Carex acutiformis, form an ecologically interesting community at the edges of the floodplain.
Regional Importance			
6. Corballis Hill S 82 87 23 ha	Woodland(d)	Ecological	Corballis Hill is composed of granite though there are drift deposits on its lower slopes. Heath and oakwood communities cover the hill. The wood has a rich ground flora and abundant bird life, including the nightjar. One of the few woodlands in Kildare which appears to be developing naturally.
7. Forenaghts Great N 942 198 0.1 ha	-	Geological	An interesting stratigraphy occurs in a small exposure near Poulaphuca. A thin layer of Old Red Sandstone type is seen between the Silurian greywackes and the Carboniferous limestone.
8. Liffey bank above Athgarvan N 820 110 1 ha	Grassland	Ecological (B)	Unstable slope cut from sandy patch of boulder clay by a meander of river Liffey. The slope has been colonised by an interesting flora, mainly plants of disturbed soils.
9. Mouds Bog N 78 18 550 ha	Raised bog	Ecological	A large well-preserved eastern raised bog near climatic limit, one of the best examples of its type. Well-developed surface topography and vegetation, including some rare species in abundance. Supports a relatively high population of grouse. The vegetation has recently been burnt.

Name of Area	Habitat	Interest	Description
KILDARE			
Regional Importance			
10. Red Bog N 976 170 4 ha	Fen Lake	Ecological	A eutrophic lake, lying between morainic ridges. Around the edges, a dense growth of aquatic and fen vegetation is invading the water surface. Bogbean, _Menyanthes_, is abundant with a floating liverwort, _Riccia fluitans_. An incipient raised bog occurs at one end of the lake.
11. Royal Canal 0 000 375 10 km section	River	Ecological	Contact area between different river systems. Interesting flora with several unusual species present.
Local Importance			
12. Ballynafagh Lake N81 28 31 ha	Lake	Ecological(O)	Shallow artificial lake with patches of emergent vegetation in the middle as well as around the shore. Rich wildfowl feeding area and breeding site for many waterbirds, some found nowhere else in the county.
13. Carrighill Quarry N 804 051 0.5 ha	–	Geological	Type section of the rarely exposed Carrighill Formation (Lower Palaeozoic).
14. Derryvullagh Island N 688 006 3 ha	Woodland(d)	Ecological(B)	Low drift island, surrounded by raised bog, with young woodland composed of hawthorn, blackthorn, elder, hazel and a few trees of privet. Several rare plant species occur, e.g. toothwort, _Lathraea squamaria_. Bird life of the area is rich.
15. Donadea Wood N 83 32 250 ha	Woodland(d)	Ecological	The woodland provides an exceptionally good contrast between different types of forest. Planted ash, sycamore, oak and beech occur with some natural hawthorn, hazel and elder as well as spruce and larch. Has a moderately rich bird life and a wide range of mammals.
16. Dunlavin Marshes N 85 03 26 ha (also in Wicklow)	Marsh Fen	Ecological	A large area of fen and marsh occurring amongst moraines. The flora is diverse and interesting and is calcicole in nature.
17. Glen Ding N 963 155 4 ha (also in Wicklow)	–	Geomorphological	A dry glacial spillway which has extensive deltaic deposits in surrounding areas.
18. Grand Canal N 97 29 N 65 31 40 km section	River	Ecological	A waterbody of botanical and ecological importance, since it brings aquatic communities into otherwise monotonous farmland. The flora and fauna is comparatively rich being recruited from many different feeder streams.

Name of Area	Habitat	Interest	Description
KILDARE			
Local Importance			
19. Kilteel Wood N 980 216 4 ha	Woodland(d)	Ecological	Small area of remnant oak scrub on Ordovician rock which was formerly coppiced. The wood is now open and is not regenerating. The ground flora is species poor.
20. Liffey at Osberstown N 870 208 0.5 ha	Woodland(d)	Ecological (B)	Steep riverbank with wet boulder clay covered by mosses, willows and woodland herbs. Several interesting species occur.
21. Louisa Bridge N 995 368 3 ha	Marsh	Ecological	A terraced area of marsh extending from the Royal Canal to banks of the Rye Water. Iron-rich spring gives rise to specialised habitat conditions with interesting plant and insect communities.
22. Moorhill N 88 07 19 ha	–	Geological Geomorphological	Rare sedimentary features in inverted greywacke beds are exposed in this glacial spillway.
23. Poulaphuca Gorge N 930 080 5 ha (also in Wicklow)	Exposed rock	Ecological(B)	Steep slopes cut in Ordovician schists by the R.Liffey.The slopes of the gorge have been colonised by trees, predominantaly beech. Several unusual plants occur.
24. Prosperous Bog N 83 29 11 ha	Raised bog	Ecological	Raised bog with a representative and fairly rich flora but modified by fire. Some typical surface features are developed.
25. Rye Water Valley N 95 37 42 ha	Woodland(d) Lake	Ecological(B,O)	Damp woodland and river banks with a relatively rich flora including two unusual plant species, the St. John's wort, _Hypericum hirsutum_, and the figwort, _Scrophularia auriculata_. Rich in passerines and waterbirds, including wintering wildfowl.
26. Slate quarries N 99 19 14 ha	–	Geological	A good section of the local Ordovician grey-wackes occurs here.
27. Usk marshes N 84 02 30 ha	Marsh	Ecological	Small calcareous marshes overlooked by a high esker. Both habitats have a well-developed flora and the marsh a relatively large number of snipe.

Name of Area	Habitat	Interest	Description

International Importance

1. Kiltorcan old quarries S 559 343 1 ha	–	Geological	Two small shallow quarries exhibit strata rich in animal and plant fossils of the upper Devonian. It is a type locality for many species.

National Importance

2. Dunmore cave S 509 650 0.5 km section	–	Geomorphological	Series of Upper Carboniferous limestone caves, with well-developed dripstone formations. The passages are broad and mostly dry.
3. Thomastown S 580 409 6 ha	Grassland	Ecological(B)	A riverside meadow with two rare plant species characteristic of the Nore valley. These are the autumn crocus, _Colchicum autumnale_, and nettle-leaved bell flower, _Campanula trachelium_. River channel and swamp both hold large invertebrate populations.

Regional Importance

4. Archer's Grove quarry S 517 548 0.2 ha	–	Geological	The original quarry where the Kilkenny black marble was excavated. The rock is a dark limestone with some fossils.
5. Ballykeefe Wood S 41 51 60 ha	Woodland(d)	Ecological	A small oakwood on the slopes of the Slieve Ardagh Hills. It has been managed in the past and has a complex path system inside. Some areas show a good succession from heath and rough grazing that was formerly open ground. The area is a Nature Reserve.
6. Ballylogue Wood S 676 325 8 ha	Woodland(d)	Ecological	The wood is predominantly of oak with some ash and birch in the high canopy. Understorey of holly and hazel. Typical ground flora for damp oakwood, similar to that in Kylecorragh Wood (see below).
7. Brownstown Wood S 66 30 17 ha	Woodland(d)	Ecological	Oakwood on an acid brown earth soil with a high canopy of oak and a mixed understorey of birch, rowan and some holly.
8. Garryrickin woods S 40 38 31 ha	Woodland(d)	Ecological	These two small deciduous woods occur in a larger area of plantations on the northwest slope below Windgap. They have been developing naturally for a considerable time and consist of oak, hazel and some birch. Both are included in the Garryrickin Nature Reserve.
9. Hugginstown Fen S 52 30 47 ha	Fen	Ecological(B)	A large isolated area of fen and swamp with a variety of plant communities and several uncommon plants. The sedge _Carex diandra_, not recorded elsewhere in the county, is abundant. Other uncommon species found are the bur-marigold, _Bidens cernua_, the St. John's wort, _Hypericum elodes_ and water dropwort, _Oenanthe fistulosa_.

Plate 18: Dunmore Cave, Co. Kilkenny where lime-rich drainage water
has coated the rocks with calcium carbonate. The
stalagmite on the right may have taken tens of thousands
of years to form but the straw stalactites at top left
take only a few years to form, falling off when they get
too heavy (Kilkenny 2).

Plate 19: A modified part of the Abbeyleix woodlands, Co. Laois.
The openness of the ground layer with few tree seedlings
and no shrub growth are highly unnatural features, along
with the beech tree to the right of the path (Laois 1).

Name of Area	Habitat	Interest	Description
KILKENNY			
Regional Importance			
10. Kylecorragh Wood S 68 30 41 ha	Woodland(d)	Ecological	An area of damp relict oak woodland with fairly steep slopes in the valley of the river Nore. Canopy almost entirely composed of oak with some sycamore. Understorey of holly, hazel, and blackthorn in places. Diverse and rich ground flora. Little or no regeneration.
11. Kyleadohir Wood S 37 42 66 ha	Woodland(d)	Ecological	Old estate woodland, mostly of oak, established on a former field system close to the King's River. The soil is a wet clay and the ground flora reflects this feature. The area is a Nature Reserve.
12. Lough Cullin 61 18 250 ha	Lake Fen	Ecological(O)	A small lake surrounded by extensive areas of marsh, fen, bog and swamp showing the successional stages of the hydrosere very clearly. With the exception of three small lakes near Johnstown and the Castlecomer lakes, Lough Cullin is the only area of permanent still water in the county. Moderate numbers of duck occur in winter.
13. Tibberaghny Marshes S 44 21 150 ha	Grassland	Ecological(O)	An area of swamp, marshes and wet fields beside the Suir river , important for wintering duck particularly teal, mallard and wigeon. Greylag geese occasionally occur.
Local Importance			
14. Ardaloo fen S 46 62 38 ha	Fen	Ecological	A large area of swamp dominated by reed, Phragmites, and surrounded by marshy fields with an interesting flora. It is situated at Threecastles where the Dinin River meets the Nore.
15. Bennettsbridge S 553 477 1 ha	Grassland	Ecological(B)	A small damp unmanaged pasture with interesting communities. The rich calcicole flora includes many orchid species. Some blackthorn scrub occurs.
16. Castlecomer Estate S 54 75 S 54 72 250 ha	Woodland(m)	Ecological	Areas of neglected estate woodlands and small lakes, originally planted and maintained for ornamental purposes. Trees include exotic conifers and ornamental shrubs as well as native species of oak, ash and hazel. The area provides a refuge for many plant and animal species.
17. Fiddown Island S 47 20 22 ha	Marsh	Ecological(B)	A low-lying river island completely covered with reedswamp and willow. An interesting variety of willow species and their various hybrids occurs here.

Name of Area	Habitat	Interest	Description
KILKENNY			
Local Importance			
18. Granny quarries S 57 14 0.2 ha.	-	Geological	Good sections of the lower Hook Head rocks (see Wexford) are exposed near Granny, north of Waterford.
19. The Loughans S 31 63 26 ha	Grassland	Ecological	An area of low-lying calcareous meadows and winter wet pastures. Rich calcareous grassland with several uncommon species.
20. Tullanvooly Bog S 29 69 12 ha	Fen	Ecological(B)	An area of bog and fen with several uncommon plants including the fly orchid, _Ophrys insectifera_.
21. Urlingford scrub S 33 64 73 ha	Woodland(d)	Ecological	The area is a hillside dominated by hazel scrub with few other woody species. It is a fine, representative patch of this type of community.
22. Whitehall quarries S 64 62 13 ha	Grassland	Ecological(B)	The floors and surrounding areas of these two disused quarries harbour interesting plant communities.

Name of Area	Habitat	Interest	Description

LAOIS

National Importance

1. Abbeyleix Woods S 42 82 120 ha	Woodland(d)	Ecological	Woods of well-grown oak, <u>Quercus robur</u>, on either side of the Nore. The soil is deep and often wet and the shrub and ground flora very well-developed. The area has good habitat diversity and is one of the most important woods in the Midlands. A few small reed-fringed lakes of some value to wildfowl **are** included.
2. Timahoe eskers S 54 92 38 ha	Woodland(d)	Ecological Geomorphological	One of the best examples of esker ridges in the country showing branching and other characteristic features . Western part is covered by hazel woodland but is being excavated. Eastern ridge partly planted by western hemlock, Japanese larch and spruce species. Hazel, oak and some ash also occur.

Regional Importance

3. Annaghmore Lough N 31 14 250 ha	Lake Marsh	Ecological	Calcicole communities occur to the north of this lake and calcifuge swamp areas to the south, as bogland approaches it. A wintering area for small numbers of wildfowl and waders.
4. Clonaslee eskers N 27 12 250 ha	Fen Grassland Marsh	Ecological(B) Geomorphological	A series of glacial esker ridges with a good variety of habitats. At the Derry Hills the eskers peter out and become partly covered by bog. Calcareous marshes here are very species-rich with butterworts, <u>Pinguicula vulgaris</u>, P. lusitanica, the clubmoss, <u>Selaginella</u>, etc. The eskers themselves also have an interesting flora including heathy areas with the vetch, <u>Vicia orobus</u>.
5. Clopook Wood S 58 90 4 ha	Woodland(d)	Ecological	Ashwood occurs around this limestone hill with hazel as an understorey.The flora of lower plants, particularly lichens, is rich and the area is of considerable interest.
6. Curragh S 35 77 400 ha	Fen Grassland	Ecological	Rough meadow, calcareous peat and raised bog with a variety of interesting communities showing succession. Small groups of white-fronted geese use the area.
7. Killeshin glen S 664 770 0.5 km section	-	Geological	An important stream section through the middle and upper Namurian,containing numerous fossils.
8. Luggacurran S 587 880 0.5 km section	-	Geological	This is an almost complete stream section in the Namurian of the Castlecomer Plateau.
9. Monettia Bog N 35 15 750 ha	Raised bog	Ecological(Z)	A good example of raised bog with typical flora and fauna, including the grasshopper <u>Stethophyma grossum</u>. The area is much modified around the edges.

Plate 20

The Rock of Dunamase, Co. Laois, one
of a series of abrupt limestone hills
on the plains near Portlaoise. It
creates an island of unmanaged
vegetation in an area of agriculture.
The photograph was taken in June when
elder, _Sambucus nigra_, is in flower
(Laois 12).

Plate 21:   Coastal grassland and blanket bog on the Atlantic slopes
            of Achill Island.   Barnacle geese from nearby islands,
            find some feeding on the more isolated parts of this
            coast.

Name of Area	Habitat	Interest	Description

LAOIS

Regional Importance

10. Moyardd stream S 565 832 1 km section	-	Geological	An excellent example of the typical lithologies of the basal Coal Measures is shown in this stream section. Many of the beds are fossiliferous.
11. Ridge of Portlaoise N 47 03 - S 49 96 90 ha	Grassland	Ecological Geomorphological	A glacial esker ridge with hazel scrub, old oaks and Scot's pine. The best section is to the south of the town, but is being excavated.
12. Rock of Dunamase S 525 985 5 ha	Rock outcrop Grassland Woodland(d)	Ecological Geomorphological	One of a series of small limestone hills, erosional features known as 'hums' above a plain. Well-developed hazel scrub and also interesting grassland communities occur in places.
13. Slieve Bloom N 29 05 400 ha	Blanket bog	Ecological	On each side of the Cut where the road goes over the ridge of the Slieve Bloom, blanket bog is found. The community is best developed in the flat sites at about 500m. The slopes below have been extensively afforested. Bird fauna is relatively rich.

Local Importance

14. Ballaghmore Bog S 18 89 250 ha	Raised bog	Ecological	A good example of a raised bog with a characteristic flora. A strong growth of heather occurs marginally, with a variety of lichens and fungi.
15. Ballylynan S 67 88 40 ha	Grassland	Ecological	Calcareous meadowland composed of a variety of coarse grasses. The area is representative of old unfertilised pasture and has considerable ecological interest because of the diversity of habitats.
16. Barrow valley at Tankardstown Bridge S 703 5 ha	Grassland	Ecological	A variety of interesting habitats occur here in the river valley with a fairly rich calcareous flora.
17. Cloonadadoran Bog S 47 92 350 ha	Raised bog	Ecological	A good example of an extensive, very wet bog with numerous pools and channels. Eastern area is being partly afforested. Large snipe population.
18. Coolroe Castle N 610 040 9 ha	Fen	Ecological(B)	Fen with small shallow streams running through it. The area has a rich flora with numerous sedge species.
19. Delour River near Lacca Manor S 29 98 20 ha	Woodland(d)	Ecological	Narrow river valley with wet pasture on western side and an oak woodland on the east.

Name of Area	Habitat	Interest	Description
LAOIS			
Local Importance			
20. Emo Court N 54 07 200 ha	Woodland(m)	Ecological	Estate woodland with a mixture of conifers and deciduous species. Lake used by small numbers of water birds.
21. Kilteale Hill S 54 99 27 ha	Exposed rock Woodland(d)	Ecological	Limestown outcrop with hazel scrub and gorse, Ulex europaeus.
22. Knockacolla quarry S 315 909 0.1 ha	-	Geological	Good examples of Carboniferous crinoids occur in the rocks of this quarry.
23. Knockaroe Bog S 29 87 54 ha	Raised bog	Ecological	A good example of a small wet bog surrounded by grassland and patches of gorse scrub.
24. Lisbigney Bog S 46 79 43 ha	Fen	Ecological(B)	A small fen with a dense stand of common reed, Phragmites, in the south-west corner. Interesting communities of sedges, Carex spp. The area supports a good population of snipe.
25. Moanavaw or 'Yellow Bog' S 51 98 26 ha	Raised bog	Ecological	Small area of raised bog bordered by swampy fields with much marsh marigold, Caltha.
26. Nore River S 35 92 76 ha	Woodland(d)	Ecological	A marshy area with hazel scrub grading into a woodland of holly, beech, birch, and oak, occurs south of Castletown.
27. Rock of Cashel S 480 920 3 ha	-	Geological	Small outcrop of limestone with characteristics of deposition in turbid environments. The rock is highly fossiliferous with crinoids and brachiopods.
28. Rossmore S 667 744 0.1 ha	-	Geological	A good exposure of a coal seam occurs in Widow Malone's quarry near Rossmore.
29. Rossagad Bog N 44 04 150 ha	Raised bog	Ecological	An extensive raised bog with typical flora.
30. The Great Heath of Portlaoise N 53 02 156 ha	Grassland Heath	Ecological	Formerly more extensive, but now a disturbed heath with a low diversity of plant species. Some areas colonised by gorse scrub, others dominated by heather with areas of grassland.

Name of Area	Habitat	Interest	Description
LEITRIM			

International Importance

Name of Area	Habitat	Interest	Description
1. Glenade Cliffs G 74 47 800 ha	Exposed rock Grassland	Ecological(B,O) Geological Geomorphological	The mountain communities of this area which adjoins Ben Bulben in Sligo are the best developed in the country and are of the greatest ecological interest. They contain an abundance of arctic-alpine species of plant which cover a substantial part of the limestone cliffs and outcrops. The species include many of restricted range e.g. the willowherb, *Epilobium alsinefolium*. The flora of lower plants ferns, mosses, and lichens is also particularly rich. Cliffs extend from Eagle's Rock, a piece of the plateau which has broken off from the main massif, almost to Glenade Lough.
a) Glenade Lough (National) G 82 46 160 ha	Lake	Ecological(B)	This lake has considerable botanical interest and aquatic vegetation is well-developed in its clear waters.
b) Arroo Mountain (National) G 83 52 120 ha	Exposed rock	Ecological(B)	The north-facing cliffs on Arroo Mountain repeat many of the same communities as in Glenade though they are not quite as varied.
2. Slieve Anierin H 013 173 0.5 km section	-	Geological	An important exposure of part of the Namurian succession occurs in the upper reaches of the Stony River. It is probably the best section of these rocks in Europe.

National Importance

Name of Area	Habitat	Interest	Description
3. Lough Gill woods G 79 34 62 ha	Woodland(d)	Ecological(B)	At the east end of the lake semi-natural woods occur on the thin limestone soils near Sriff Cottage. In Kilmore townland oak and hazel canopy prevails with a good mixture of ash, hawthorn, willows and wych elm. A rich ground flora occurs.

Regional Importance

Name of Area	Habitat	Interest	Description
4. Aghagrania River H 998 120 0.5 km section	-	Geological	A good exposure of fossiliferous Carboniferous rocks occurs in the stream bed from just below the bridge northwards.
5. Corry, L. Allen G 957 233 1 ha	-	Geological	Another fossiliferous exposure in the Carboniferous rocks of the lakeshore.
6. Glencar Waterfall G 750 430 4 ha	Exposed rock Woodland(d)	Ecological Geological	A variety of calcareous habitats occurs with communities characterised by moisture-loving organisms, particularly bryophytes and lichens. The river falls over a band of shale above an excellent exposure of the Carboniferous limestone.

Name of Area	Habitat	Interest	Description
LEITRIM			
Regional Importance.			
7. Lough Melvin G 88 53 2400 ha	Lake	Ecological(Z)	Clear water limestone lake with three varieties of trout and a race of char. Interesting marginal vegetation occurs in some places.
8. Lough Scannal N 04 90 50 ha	Lake Marsh Woodland(d)	Ecological(B,O)	The most natural and biologically interesting part of the Shannon in the county. A variety of rich habitats occurs with the characteristic Shannon flora and fauna well-developed. Wintering wildfowl including small numbers of Greenland white-fronted geese.
9. O'Donnell's Rock G 88 36 31 ha	Woodland(d)	Ecological Geological	One of the few naturally developing woods on the Sligo-Leitrim limestone mountains. Predominantly hazel with some ash, willow and oak saplings growing on the clayey talus slope. Canopy approximately 5 m high. Typical ground flora. A good section of the upper part of the Carboniferous occurs beside a track.
10. Sheemore wood G 990 040 9 ha	Woodland(d)	Ecological(B,O)	One of the purest ash-hazel wood in the country, naturally developing on the steep side of a limestone hill. Some beech trees and conifers present. Highly diverse ground flora, including bryophytes. Interesting animal and bird populations.
Local Importance			
11. Aghavoghil stream G 865 520 8 ha	Exposed rock Woodland(d)	Ecological	A river-cut gorge in the edge of a limestone plateau with a series of waterfalls, dripping rock faces and wet clay banks. Hazel scrub with hawthorn, birch and ash covers much of west bank. Ground flora similar to other wet woods.
12. Annaghearly Lough H 00 03 21 ha	Lake	Ecological(B)	A good representative of the lakes in south and central Leitrim. Two uncommon plant species occur.
13. Corduff Lough H 17 12 20 ha	Marsh	Ecological(B)	Small marsh with the uncommon sedge, <u>Carex elongata</u>.
14. Corracromph & Cashel N 07 90 40 ha	Raised bog	Ecological(O)	These are two adjacent small bogs with much bog cotton, <u>Eriophorum</u> spp. They are used by <u>c</u> 60 white-fronted geese for roosting and feeding.
15. Cromlin Bridge H 105 140 2 ha	Woodland(d)	Ecological	Small area of hazel scrub on steep calcareous drift deposits. It contains elm (much cut), with ash and willow. The site has a rich ground flora with many characteristic species.

Name of Area	Habitat	Interest	Description
LEITRIM			
Local Importance			
16. Drumhierny Wood G 95 05 25 ha	Woodland(d)	Ecological	Predominantly oak with some beech, sycamore, wych elm and an understorey of blackthorn, hazel, ash and bramble on a base-rich soil. The canopy is dense.
17. Drumod lakeshore N 04 90 15 ha	Woodland(d)	Ecological	Woods on the shore of Lough Scannal and Bofin. Alder and willow are prominant in the wetter sections, occuring in a calcareous herb community. Elsewhere ash/hazel woodland prevails with spindle tree, Euonymus .
18. Garadice Lough H 190 110 5 ha	Woodland(d)	Ecological	The deciduous woodland on the drumlin north of Cherry Island shows interesting contrasts between acid and alkaline soils. The rich ground flora includes an uncommon species of moss.
19. Kinlough Wood G 82 54 41 ha	Woodland(d)	Ecological	A planted wood on a very wet site. Alder, ash, birch, willow, hazel with some low-growing holly are the predominant species. Some regeneration occurs at margins, particularly on north side , but the wood is closely grazed in the central areas.
20. Lough Allen (Parts) G 960 175 7 ha	Woodland(d)	Ecological	Characteristic marginal vegetation of alder 'swamp forest' on the heavy clay soils. Affected and probably maintained by artificial fluctuations in lake level.
21. Lough Rinn N 10 93 100 ha	Fen Marsh	Ecological(B,O)	A series of lakes which contain outliers of the Shannon plant communities. Lough Rinn lies on limestone drift and is fringed by alders. Extensive reed beds occur at the northern end of lake and also in Loughs Errew and Sallagh.
22. Owengar Wood G 910 230 3 ha	Woodland(d)	Ecological	A small wood on wet clay soils below the Owengar Bridge with some beech and willow. Thick understorey of hawthorn, hazel and holly.
23. Ramsons Pot G 896 458 1 ha	-	Geomorphological	The main pothole is situated in a rift below L. Adunny, 20 m long and 8 m deep. It is about 30 m deep itself and receives two streams. Some cave passages also exist.
24. Teampall Shetric G 819 423 0.3 km section	-	Geomorphological	A small cave system with many vertical passages, waterfalls and streams.
25. Wild Cat's Hole G 851 465 0.1 ha	-	Geological Geomorphological	A section through interesting evaporatic rocks of the Carboniferous is exposed here.

Name of Area	Habitat	Interest	Description
LIMERICK			
National Importance			
1. Aughinish Island (E) R 28 53 79 ha	–	Geological	Lower Carboniferous reef limestones in which knoll forms can be studied in approximately their original position. Well-preserved transitions occur from the knolls to off-bank facies.
2. Aughinish-Askeaton shore R 31 53 550 ha	Mudflats Grassland	Ecological(B,O)	Probably the third most important section of the Shannon estuary for its shorebirds. Wildfowl average 2,900, mostly wigeon and teal, waders 3,500. Numbers of teal and curlew are of international importance, scaup, redshank and bar-tailed godwit of national significance. Poularone Creek and Deel estuary are the richest sites. The coastal outcrops of limestone have considerable botanical interest and their communities are outliers of the Burren flora.
3. Ballinacurra Creek R 54 55 49 ha	Marsh(s)	Ecological(B)	A well-developed brackish marsh extends down the Shannon estuary in front of the embankments. It consists of reeds, Phragmites, up to 4 m high and is unique in Ireland because of the occurence of the clubrush, Scirpus triquetrus. Other species found on these muddy shores are the bulrush, Typha angustifolia, scurvy grass, Cochlearia anglica and summer snowflake, Leucojum. All in all the plant community is most unusual.
4. Ballylanders/ Kilfinnane moraine R 59 20 - R 77 25 13 km section	–	Geomorphological	A very good example of the south Irish end moraine, produced by the furthest extension of ice during the glacial age.
5. Foynes Island R 26 53 16 ha	–	Geological	Exposure of Clare shales containing the type localities for two goniatite fossil species.
6. Linfield quarry R 752 465 0.5 ha	–	Geological	Quarry section of columnar basalt displaying a circular 'sunburst' structure at the eastern end. This 'sunburst' structure is probably unique in Ireland.
7. Lough Gur R 64 41 100 ha	Fen Lake Marsh	Ecological(B,O) Geological	A varied wetland area has been produced by a former drop in lake level. There are several basins separated by steep hills in which good reef limestones are exposed at intervals. The lake is eutrophic with a rich flora and invertebrate fauna which provides a good food supply for wintering wildfowl. Coot (920), wigeon (1,200), teal(600), shoveler (440) and tufted duck (450) are the most numerous. Important also for breeding wildfowl. One of the major sites for sub-fossil remains of the giant Irish deer.

Name of Area	Habitat	Interest	Description
LIMERICK			
Regional Importance			
8. Askeaton quarry R 340 500 0.5 ha	–	Geological	A quarry with good exposures of the lower part of the Carboniferous limestones.
9. Aughinish Island(W) R 276 531 1 ha	Marsh(s)	Ecological(O)	A small area of wet grassland and standing water used as a feeding and roosting area by wintering and migrating shorebirds. Mallard, teal, wigeon and white-fronted geese are important.
10. Barigone R 300 506 8 ha	Exposed rock Grassland	Ecological(B)	An area of grassland and bare limestone with isolated shrubs. The flora is an outlier of that characteristic of the Burren in northern Clare. It includes the flax, Linum bienne and violet, Viola hirta, as well as the more frequent species.
11. Caherconlish quarry R 682 501 1 ha	–	Geological	Quarry section showing fine exposure of columnar trachyte. The columns are approximately 1 m diameter and 10 m high. This is the first site of a series in Limerick which illustrate the only major centre of volcanicity in the country.
12. Carrigogunnel R 498 552 1 ha	–	Geological	Rocky knoll in which pyroclastic ashes overlie a basalt lava flow, which in turn overlies Carboniferous limestone.
13. Cromwell and Kilteely Hills R 73 40 300 ha	–	Geological	Cromwell Hill consists of lavas overlying the Carboniferous limestons, while Kilteely Hill has exposures of more varied volcanic rocks.
14. Curraghturk R 28 21 200 ha	–	Geomorphological	Small glacial spillway representing the highest of those formed by the lake that once filled the Glen of Aherlow.
15. Derk Hill R 76 42 400 ha	–	Geological	It shows the whole of the Limerick volcanic area in microcosm and is consequently of considerable interest.
16. Galbally R 798 280 40 ha	–	Geomorphological	A glacial meltwater channel occurs here at the west of the Glen of Aherlow with associated delta remnants.
17. Glenastar Wood R 24 38 16 ha	Woodland(d)	Ecological	A dense woodland in a deep, wet, V-shaped valley. High canopy formed by oak. Birch, hazel and ash also present with a characteristic ground flora.

Name of Area	Habitat	Interest	Description
LIMERICK			
Regional Importance			
18. Glen Bog R 66 38 12 ha	Fen Woodland(d)	Ecological	A cut-over bog, now covered with dense alder/willow scrub or carr with some open patches of standing water and reeds.
19. Glenstal R 74 56 3 ha	Exposed rock Woodland(d)	Ecological(B)	A wet wooded valley on the side of the Slievefelim mountains, it contains much of ecological interest. Mosses and ferns occur in variety and the bird cherry, _Prunus padus_, in the wet woodland.
20. Kilmeedy R 365 292 0.1 ha	-	Geological	An important rock stratum, the Ballyvergin shale, is exposed in the County Council quarry.
21. Knockderc Hill R 66 31 2 ha	-	Geological	Quarry in red syenite.
22. Knockseefin Hill R 75 45 150 ha	-	Geological	Pyroclastic succession lying on top of limestone. Of considerable general and educational interest.
Local Importance			
23. Ballinvirick marsh R 391 479 1 ha	Marsh	Ecological(B)	A well developed marsh vegetation in which marsh helleborine, _Epipactis palustris_, is strongly established.
24. Ballymorrisheen R 37 47 24 ha	Fen	Ecological	An area of fen and small ponds surrounded by vegetation of common reed, _Phragmites_, and saw sedge, _Cladium_.
25. Ballyvogue fen R 385 515 6 ha	Fen	Ecological	A small area of fen characteristic of the low-lying limestone regions of the county.
26. Cappagh fen R 38 46 11 ha	Fen Marsh	Ecological	Another area of marsh and fen with an interesting diversity of plant communities.
27. Clare Glen R 735 598 1 ha (also in Tipperary N)	Woodland(d)	Ecological(B)	Narrow strip of deciduous woodland bordering the river with alder, ash, oak, rowan and sycamore. The ground flora is rich in lower plants because of the humidity.
28. Gorteennamrock R 38 48 10 ha	Marsh Fen	Ecological	An area of marsh and fen enclosing a small, scrub-covered rocky outcrop which causes good transitional communities to develop.

Name of Area	Habitat	Interest	Description
LIMERICK			
Local Importance			
29 Heathfield Wood R 402 246 3 ha	Woodland(d)	Ecological	A small, almost pure stand of young beech with some oak, in an area with few woodlands. Regeneration of beech shrub layer with ash, holly and spruce.
30. Loughmore R 54 53 15 ha	Grassland	Ecological(0)	Wet grassland which floods in winter and provides wintering grounds for a great variety of wildfowl and waders.
31 Sturamus Island R 26 53 0.2 ha	Shingle	Ecological(0)	A tern colony(140 prs) with arctic, common and sandwich terns, occurs on this small island in the Shannon estuary.
32. Tarbert Bay R 07 47 104 ha (also in Kerry)	Mudflats	Ecological (0)	An important site for wading birds (2,000) in winter, with some wildfowl (600).

Name of Area	Habitat	Interest	Description
LONGFORD			
National Importance			
1. Carrickboy quarry N 20 65 12 ha	–	Geological	A complex Carboniferous site with two reef knolls visible, one above the other. The rocks are fossiliferous and are the type locality for a bivalve species.
2. Lough Forbes and Castleforbes demesne N 09 82 400 ha	Grassland Woodland(d)	Ecological(O)	A large lake on the Shannon system fringed with reeds and woodlands. Outstanding for woodland birds, including several less common species. Important also for wintering wildfowl, particularly white-fronted geese of which up to 400 have been recorded and there are usually 200 - 300 present. It is the second most important wintering site for the species after the Wexford Slobs. The area includes Killeen Bog, a roosting ground for the geese.
3. Lough Kinale and Derragh Lough N 39 81 320 ha (also in Cavan/ Westmeath)	Lake	Ecological(O)	Lake fringed along western shore with reedswamp, and wet meadow land. Large numbers of wildfowl wintering on the lake are principal interest. Tufted duck (2,200) and pochard (2,400) have sometimes been recorded, a very high number for such a small area. A good diversity of breeding species also occurs.
4. Lough Ree N 01 53 3870 ha (also in Roscommon and Westmeath)	Lake	Ecological(O,Z)	The second largest Midland lake and probably the one least affected by eutrophication. There are many sites of interest on its islands and shores. The lake itself has a distinct fauna, with the fish pollan, at one of its two Irish sites. There is also an abundance of the glacial relict shrimp, <u>Mysis relicta</u>. Wildfowl have totalled 3,700 in winter, including tufted duck (1,700) and wigeon (1,100) but the regular population is not well known.
a) Barley Harbour-Portanure Lodge (National) N 02 56 80 ha	Marsh	Ecological(B,O)	The wildfowl habitat is excellent on this stretch of the shore and the variety in vegetation and habitat makes it of considerable ecological importance. Marsh and woodland are important for nesting birds. Sheltered bays contain some of the only reedbeds on the lake.
b) Curreen Wood (Local) N 00 67 47 ha	Woodland(d)	Ecological	Old woodland dominated by oak, <u>Quercus robur</u>, with some sycamore and holly. The ground flora has some interest.
c) Arnee Pt-R. Inny (Local) N 10 55 60 ha	Grassland	Ecological(O)	A valuable site for breeding and wintering birds. It is used by mallard, teal and tufted duck and sometimes by white-fronted geese. Many waders occur, including black-tailed godwit (200) on migration and golden plover.

Name of Area	Habitat	Interest	Description
LONGFORD			
Regional Importance			
5. Ardagullion quarry N 303 768 0.1 ha	-	Geological	A disused quarry showing a section through Carboniferous basinal rocks. Many sedimentary features are well seen.
6. Cloondara bog N 08 74 250 ha	Raised bog	Ecological	A fine example of a midland raised bog with a typical flora and well-developed pool and hummock complex.
7. Cloonshinnagh bog N 30 75 320 ha	Raised bog	Ecological	A large and well-developed raised bog with a characteristic flora.
8. Cordara & Fortwilliam N 03 64 N 02 63 22 ha	Turlough	Ecological(O)	These two small areas support up to 1,000 aquatic birds in winter if the water level is at a certain height. Cordara is the more important turlough.
9. Derry Lough N 10 60 23 ha	Fen	Ecological	The fen vegetation at the north end of the lake is of some interest and includes some quaking areas. Derry Lough is calcareous, with peat linking it to the bog on the west side.
10. Derrymacar Lough N 09 58 105 ha	Lake	Ecological	A lake fringed by common reed with raised bog to the west and grassland and scrub to the east. Important wildfowl wintering area, especially for teal and mallard; also some waders - curlew, lapwing and golden plover.
11. Ferskill reefknoll N 312 790 4 ha	-	Geological	Reef-knoll of dark calcite mudstone with fauna of crinoids marking the high Visean succession.
12. Glen Lough N 27 66 90 ha (also in Westmeath)	Lake Marsh Grassland	Ecological(B,O)	A shallow lake which dries out in summer. An interesting flora occurs on the muddy lakebed and on the surrounding shores (including limestone outcrops). Used by dabbling duck, especially teal and wigeon in winter and by white-fronted geese. Large numbers (200) of wild swans occur at intervals.
13. Killoe Quarry N 197 780 8 ha	-	Geological	A small quarry below the church exposes a reef-knoll with horizontal bands of micritic limestone.
14. Lough Bannow N 03 69 80 ha	Fen	Ecological	Small area of open water choked with common reed, _Phragmites_, and developing into fen. Scattered birch and alder trees to east. Attractive wetland for waterfowl.

Name of Area	Habitat	Interest	Description
LONGFORD			
Local Importance			
15. Lough Gowna N 28 29 750 ha (also in Cavan)	Lake	Ecological(B,O)	A shallow lake set amongst drumlins and raised bogs on the R. Erne system. It has a relatively low base status, which allows aquatic plants such as quillwort, _Isoetes lacustris_, to grow in a pH of 7.5. The lake holds small populations of wildfowl in winter, especially wigeon (360), goldeneye (50) and wild swan (60), but is perhaps more important as a breeding area. A woodland fringe covers part of the shore with willow, alder and ash.
a) Erne Head N 27 87 26 ha	Woodland(d)	Ecological(O)	At Erne Head oak forms a canopy at about 25m. Beech is spreading and its young trees form an understorey, with some holly and hazel. The ground flora is acidic in character with woodrush, _Luzula sylvatica_, important. Many species of woodland birds occur, including both blackcap and garden warbler.
16. Lough Naback N 24 95 12 ha	Lake	Ecological(Z)	An acid upland lake at 128 m containing a race of char, and surrounded by upland grassland communities.
17. Mount Jessop and Derrymore bogs N 13 70 300 ha	Raised bog	Ecological	A good example of raised bog subject to intermittent burning and therefore, with short heather, _Calluna_, and many lichens, _Cladonia_.
18. Newtown reef-knoll N 266 635 4 ha	-	Geological	Low reef-knoll of dark calcite mudstone with abundant fossils.
19. Royal Canal N 234 598 N 123 637 N 168 585 15 km section	River	Ecological	Much of the canal in the county is unnavigable as it has been colonized by reed, _Phragmites_, and the clubrush, _Scirpus lacustris_. The canal now provides an undisturbed habitat for several interesting aquatic plants and animals.

Name of Area	Habitat	Interest	Description

LOUTH

International Importance

1. Dundalk Bay
J 09 07
4400 ha

Mudflats

Ecological(O)

Saltmarsh and mudflats with full range of plant communities from eel grass, *Zostera*, and cord grass, *Spartina*, to rushes, *Juncus gerardii* and grass *Puccinellia* spp. One of the most important areas in Ireland for wintering and migrating wading birds with up to 48,000 waders in whole area. With areas south, Lurgangreen, Annagassan, Dundalk Bay is of international significance for the following wading birds during different parts of the winter: oystercatcher (27,000) bar-tailed godwit (7,000), dunlin(12,000), golden plover (13,000), curlew (4,500), redshank (4,000) and knot (8,000).

a) Castlebellingham shore
0 070 977
2 km section

Shingle

Ecological(B)
Geomorphological

North of Castlebellingham the shingle-covered raised beach has a rich and varied flora and at Dromiskin the coastal plain shows the finest sequence of raised beaches in Ireland.

2. Tullyallen quarry
O 07 76
2 ha

Geological

An exposure of glacio-marine sediments and two tills occur above limestone with well-preserved solution pipes. The site is of major importance in the estimation of sea levels during the Ice Age and has yielded the only Palaeolithic remains (a stone implement) in the country. This was probably washed into place from the Irish Sea Basin rather than produced on the site.

National Importance

3. Carlingford Mountain
J 17 13
300 ha

Exposed rock

Ecological(B)

The granite summit and areas above 330 m have a diverse flora including arctic-alpine communities with a number of rare plants.

4. Clogher Head
O 18 85
40 ha

Heath

Ecological(B)
Geological

Promontory of Silurian greywackes with thin covering of shallow soil. Four uncommon plant species occur, including an abundance of squill, *Scilla verna*. A marine washing limit is excellently shown in the north of the site where the finer material has been removed from a former shoreline. This is an important Quarternary erosional feature.

5. Drakestown
N 949 868
8 ha

−

Geological

A disused quarry is cut into the lowest part of the Carboniferous at this site. The rock type is a micrite and the strata include very well-developed sedimentary features.

6. Greenore
J 225 105
1 km section

−

Geomorphological

A raised beach 3-5m higher than the existing beach and dating from the post-Mesolithic period. It shows elastic recovery of the land after the ice had retreated and also contains archaeological remains (rolled flint implements).

Name of Area	Habitat	Interest	Description
LOUTH			
Regional Importance			
7. Boyne Estuary O 14 78 250 ha	Mudflats	Ecological(O)	A river estuary much modified by canalisation. The mudflats are used by wintering wildfowl and waders, mainly below Mornington. The black-tailed godwit population at 250 is the largest on the east coast outside Wexford and there are also considerable numbers of curlew(580).
a) Baltray dunes O 15 77 150 ha (also in Meath)	Sand dunes Saltmarsh	Ecological(B,Z)	The estuary is guarded on the north side by the Baltray dune system which consists of highly calcareous, stable dunes with a good diversity of habitats. Several plant species of interest occur as well as the Mediterranean snail _Theba pisana_, which is not found outside Louth, Meath and north Dublin.
8. Carlingford Lough J 18 14 1780 ha	Sea inlet Mudflats	Ecological(O)	A large flock of scaup (1,000), about 25% of the Irish population, feeds here in winter. Other wildfowl occur on the south shore where narrow mudflats exist.
9. Collon N 99 81 0.1 ha	-	Geological	A valuable exposure of the Ordovician stratigraphy occurs with the Caradocian shelly fauna well-developed.
10. Mapastown N 989 949 0.5 ha	-	Geomorphological	Fossiliferous outwash gravel containing igneous rock derived from the north.
11. Mellifont Abbey O 01 84 150 ha	Woodland(d)	Ecological(B,Z)	A wet secondary woodland consisting of ash, alder and birch with a shrub layer of rhododendron and guelder rose. A shallow lake with alder, bulrush and bogbean around margins is also included. Rich communities containing wintergreen, _Pyrola_ sp and the Pyrenean snail, _Semilimax pyrenaicus_.
12. Slieve Gullion ring dyke J 183 102 6 ha	-	Geological	Two quarries and a number of surface exposures show the relationship between the central cone sheet(plug) and the surrounding dyke material. The hill is also a classic demonstration of crag and tail, where a hard rock outcrop has allowed glacial material to accumulate behind it.
Local Importance			
13. Ardee Bog N 93 91 300 ha	Raised bog	Ecological(B)	Cutaway raised bog on which remnants of original flora persist. A number of interesting plant species are found especially where calcareous influence from the underlying marl occurs.
14. Ballymascanlon Estuary J 08 10 80 ha	Marsh(s)	Ecological	A diversity of habitats - particularly salt and brackish marshes - occur on either side of the River Flurrey as it meanders into the estuary. The site adjoins Dundalk Bay and is used by some of the shore birds there.

Name of Area	Habitat	Interest	Description
LOUTH			
Local Importance			
15. Blackhall O 13 83 50 ha	Woodland(d)	Ecological(B)	Planted woodland composed of ash, chestnut and beech. The area has an interesting bryophyte flora.
16. Castlecoo Hill O 145 830 5 ha	Exposed rock	Ecological(B)	Rocky outcrop which is covered with heath vegetation dominated by bramble and gorse.
17. Darver Castle O 010 988 5 ha	Woodland(d)	Ecological	Small woodland consisting mainly of beech, alder, hawthorn and ash but with a diverse ground flora. Rhododendron is spreading in the wood.
18. Drumcah & Cortial Loughs H 96 06 82 ha	Fen	Ecological	Three shallow lakes amongst drumlins in the headwaters of the River Fane. The water area is now much reduced and each has an extensive development of fen and marsh around it which is tending to bog in a few places. Quaking areas based on bogbean, <u>Menyanthes</u>, occur and both waterlilies, <u>Nuphar</u> and <u>Nymphaea</u>, are found.
19. Dunany Point O 160 918 1.5 km section	-	Geomorphological	A marine headland composed of large rock fragments and boulder clay deposited as an end moraine during a re-advance of the ice in the Pleistocene period.
20. Ferry Hill J 123 193 10 ha	Woodland(d)	Ecological(B)	Mainly beech with some oak, sycamore, holly and a typical ground flora. The variety of ferns occuring here is notable.
21. Liscarragh marsh J 19 06 14 ha	Fen	Ecological	Marsh with typical fauna and flora dominated by common reed, <u>Phragmites</u>.
22. Park woodlands Omeath J 13 18 20 ha	Woodland(d)	Ecological	One of the few stands of birch in the county. Alder is also present with a ground flora dominated by bracken, <u>Pteridium</u>.
23. Reaghstown marsh N 91 99 30 ha	Fen	Ecological	Wetland with typical fauna and mixed calcicole and calcifuge flora. Willow scrub is widespread in area.
24. Stephenstown Wood J 01 03 20 ha	Woodland(m)	Ecological	Mixed deciduous and coniferous planted woodland with a typical ground flora and invertebrate fauna.
25. Trumpet Hill J 10 10 65 ha	Woodland(d)	Ecological(B)	Basalt hill with a diversity of habitats, including heath and beech woodland. Lower plants are of interest also.

Name of Area	Habitat	Interest	Description

MAYO

International importance

1. Bellacorick flush F 96 21 30 ha	Fen	Ecological (B)	An iron-rich spring and fen in blanket bog. Unusual plant communities representing a habitat which was formerly widespread but has been much grown over by peatland. Plant species include the only known site of the marsh saxifrage, _Saxifraga hirculus,_ in the Republic and the post -glacial mosses, _Camptothecium nitens_ and _Meesia tristicha_ (only Irish site). Good vegetation zonation. Fauna unstudied but probably interesting.
2. Clare Island cliffs L 66 86 150 ha	Exposed rock	Ecological (B,O Z)	Arctic-alpine plant communities of large extent with several rare species, including a hybrid saxifrage. Type locality for many invertebrate organisms because of former intensive research. Important breeding colony of seabirds, especially fulmar (1,320 prs) kittiwake (1,540 prs), razorbill (1,800 prs), guillemot (860 birds) and puffin (at least 90). Gannets first nested in 1978, Ireland's fourth gannetry.
3. Clew Bay L 91 89 11,000 ha	-	Geomorphological	The classical drowned drumlin landscape showing the sea's erosional action on a drumlin swarm which was laid down by the second advance of ice in the glacial period. Nowhere else is this type of landscape developed on such a scale nor with such variation.
4. Glenamoy F 89 35 200 ha	Blanket bog	Ecological	The most researched site on Irish low level blanket bog. Type locality for some invertebrates. Site for ecological studies associated with the International Biological Programme (1969 - 1972).
5. Inishkea Islands F 56 22 330 ha	Grassland (s)	Geological Ecological (O,Z)	The islands are formed of gneiss which is well exposed in many places. They are the main wintering ground of barnacle geese in Ireland. A maximum of 2,900 have been counted, representing 60% of Irish population and 12% of Greenland breeding stock. Other wintering birds include golden plover (1,000), sanderling (200) and purple sandpipers (150). Breeding ground of dunlin (5 prs), gulls (450 prs) and black guillemots (10 prs); also large colony of grey seals, up to 500 recorded in spring haul-out. Strong maritime influence on grassland covering islands.
6. Lough Carra M 17 72 1,900 ha	Lake Fen Woodland(d)	Ecological (B,O, Z)	Best example in the country of a spring-fed limestone lake with extensive marl deposition and extreme ecological and hydrological interest. Marginal and island woods, scrubland and herb-rich grassland. At northern end of western limestones and of interest for comparison with areas to the south e.g. Burren. Largest nesting mallard population in Ireland; up to 1,940 birds present in winter. Other wintering wildfowl of national importance include shoveler (500) and gadwall (85).

Name of Area	Habitat	Interest	Description
MAYO			
International importance			
7. Loughs Conn & Cullin G 20 10 5,000 ha	Lakes	Ecological (O,Z)	Clear water lakes on limestone and granite with brown trout, salmon and a race of char. They form a feeding and nesting site for wild-fowl with mallard (100) on L. Conn and diving duck (4,000 in Autumn) on L. Cullin. The common scoter and three other duck species breed on the heathy shores and islands.
a) Pontoon woods G 21 04 (33 ha)	Woodland(d)	Ecological Geological	Woodland is especially well-developed on the granite near Pontoon though the natural oak/holly cover has been much cleared. An excellent example of Atlantic oakwood remains, however, which is species-rich in trees and shrubs, herbs and lower plants. The associated animal communities are also rich. A good granite/schist contact is exposed in the area.
b) Garry-cloonagh (Regional) G 18 16 27 ha	Grassland	Ecological (B)	The rest of the lakeshore is of open rocky grassland or peat and a lowering of lake level has exposed wide beaches on which colonisation is taking place naturally. The limestone flora is diverse and interesting with species such as the cranesbill, Geranium sanguineum and burnet, Sanguisorba officinalis, its only site in the Republic. A representative stretch of shoreline occurs at Garrycloonagh.
8. Owenduff bog F 86 07 4,150 ha	Blanket bog	Ecological	Best and largest example of intact blanket bog (low-level Atlantic type) in Mayo and probably in Ireland. Not as well investig-ated as other bogs, e.g. Glenamoy, but also far more isolated from outside influences such as forestry and agriculture.
National importance			
9. Annagh Head Scotchport F 63 35 55 ha	-	Geological	Coastal cliff section consisting of Pre-Cambrian rocks, reconstituted in two phases (before and during the Caledonian). Such examples are rare in old rocks in Ireland.
10. Cloughmoyne M 22 50 90 ha	Exposed rock	Ecological (B)	Herb-rich grassland on limestone ridge with colonies of the fern, Gymnocarpium robertianum, in cracks in rock, the only known site in Ireland. Other species of interest include wood bitter-vetch, Vicia orobus.
11. Dooaghtry L 73 69 500 ha	Grassland Marsh(s)	Ecological (B,O)	The area includes dunes, calcareous grassland, oak/birch woodland, three lakes, marsh and saltmarsh which support varied plant and animal communities. The wide occurrence of windblown sand, the presence of temporary stream channels and of seasonally flooded grassland are interesting habitat features. The shallow lakes and marshes are used by a great variety of wintering wildfowl and waders and passage migrants, in particular barnacle geese (30), whooper and Bewick's swans (25), duck (250), and golden plover (400).
12. Finny bridle path M 005 594 0.1 ha	-	Geological	Early Ordovician or Cambrian graptolites occur in an outcrop here, the oldest fossil-bearing horizon in the west of Ireland.

Name of Area	Habitat	Interest	Description
MAYO			
National Importance			
13. Illanmaster F 94 44 17 ha	Grassland	Ecological (O)	Site of important breeding colony of puffins (at least 2,000 prs), largest in Connaught. Large numbers of storm petrels also present in breeding season. A few barnacle geese (50) visit the island in winter.
14. Inishglora F 61 31 41 ha	Exposed rock	Ecological (O)	Seabird breeding colony. Large numbers of storm petrels (10,000 prs) nest the most important site in the country outside the south-west; also 80 prs of common, herring and great black-backed gulls.
15. Lough Mask M 1,140 8,000 ha	Lake	Ecological (Z)	A deep lake with well-developed stratification in summer. Fauna includes the shrimp, _Niphargus_ and the glacial relict fish, char, _Salvelinus_. The lake supports a low density of wintering wildfowl, for example, mallard (190), wigeon (350), and tufted duck (360).
a) L. Mask shoreline (National) M 14 64 915 ha	Grassland Exposed rock	Ecological (B) Geological	Lough Mask is situated on the junction of Silurian slates and Carboniferous limestone and on the east side much limestone is exposed. It forms a highly dissected shoreline with pavement, scrub and grassland. The rocks near Ballygarry and Clonbur are especially interesting geologically. The vegetation is species-rich and changing under a currently reduced level of grazing.
b) Owenbrin (National) M05 60 46 ha	Grassland Marsh	Ecological (B)	The flat unfenced acid grassland at the mouth of the Owenbrin River contrasts with that across the lake. Winding streams produce variations in a plant cover of great ecological value. The plant species include chamomile, _Anthemis nobilis_, allseed, _Radiola_ and the St. John's worts, _Hypericum elodes_ and _H. canadense_. The site is also used by migrating wading birds.
c) Barnarinnia (Regional) M 06 60 70 ha	Woodland (d)	Ecological	On the west side a large oakwood occurs but is heavily overgrazed at the moment. It has many natural features, however.
d) Ballykine (Regional) M 11 56 30 ha	Woodland (d)	Ecological	The natural scrub on much of the eastern and south eastern shore gives way to a well-grown stand of oak at Ballykine, surrounded by coniferous plantings.
e) Cong area (Regional) M 13 58 8 ha	-	Geological	The waters of Lough Mask flow entirely underground to Lough Corrib and parts of the streamways can be seen, together with many small caves. A little-explored area.

Name of Area	Habitat	Interest	Description

MAYO

National Importance

16. Mweelrea
L 79 67
700 ha

Exposed rock
Heath

Ecological (B)
Geological

The fine Ordovician greywacke cliffs on the north side carry high-level communities with some unusual species. The largest stands of Mediterranean heath, _Erica erigena_, in Ireland grow on the south side above Kilary Harbour. Here they are unusually isolated from agriculture and must contain their characteristic fauna, though this has not been investigated.

17. Old Head
L83 82
29 ha

Woodland (d)

Ecological

A rare example of Atlantic oakwood situated on the coast, with a rich growth of lichens. Typical invertebrates, as yet poorly known. Oasis for birdlife, breeding species have included redstart and nightjar.

18. Termoncarragh Lake
F 66 34
150 ha

Marsh

Ecological (B,O)

The site includes well-developed sand dunes with an interesting flora and a lagoonal lake with eutrophic, species-rich marshes. Important nesting area for waders (dunlin, lapwing, snipe and red-necked phalarope in past). Also used by wintering wildfowl including mallard (100), tufted duck (200), mute swan (74), whooper swan (180), sometimes white-fronted and barnacle geese and golden plover (3,000).

Regional Importance

19. Aille River cave
M 07 81
1 ha

–

Geological

The Aille River rises on sandstone and sinks when it meets limestone, south-east of Westport. The site is a wooded cliff and the water inside the cave is very deep. It slips sideways into a bedding plane near the surface.

20. Belderg Harbour
F 995 415
3 km section

–

Geological

An interesting coastal section showing the development of deformational curvilinear folds in Pre-Cambrian rocks.

21. Bills Rocks
L 550 935
3 ha

Exposed rock

Ecological (O)

Seabird breeding colonies on tiny rocky islands. Puffin (1,000 prs), razorbill (100 prs), kittiwake (175 prs), and a few guillemots, gulls, shags and oystercatchers are found. Barnacle geese graze the islands in winter.

22. Burren
M 12 99
19 ha

Exposed rock

Ecological (B,O)
Geological

North-facing cliff of conglomerate with arctic-alpine communities at relatively low level. They include several plant species unknown elsewhere in north Mayo. Some cliff-nesting birds also occur. A small exposure of rock in the stream to the south of the hill has yielded mid-Devonian plant remains, some of the earliest such fossils known.

Plate 22: One of the best-grown stands of the spring flowering
mediterranean heath, _Erica erigena_, occurs at the head
of Bellacragher Bay beside Mulrany Hill, Co. Mayo. Here
it grows with gorse, _Ulex europaeus_ and young trees of
alder and hazel (Mayo 41).

Plate 23: Hog's Island in Lough Key, Co. Roscommon - one of several
tree-covered drumlins in the lake. The woodland was
planted originally but like most estate woods it is slowly
assuming a natural structure and composition, a process
that takes at least 200 years (Roscommon 27).

Name of Area	Habitat	Interest	Description
MAYO			

Regional Importance

23. Cappagh M 17 93 12 ha	-	Geomorphological Geological	Good roches moutonées, i.e. ice-smoothed rock mounds with striae. They are formed of folded Pre-Cambrian sediments which are valuable also in the teaching of structural geology.
24. Clyard kettle-holes M 22 58 30 ha	Fen Marsh	Ecological (B)	A complex low-lying area with many small lakes. Interesting and rather different vegetation is developed in adjacent basins. Some uncommon plant species occur, including floating water-dropwort, _Oenanthe fistulosa_. Diversity of insects, and some birds.
25. Carrowmore Lough F 83 28 1,000 ha	Lake Heath	Ecological (B,O)	A wintering area for wildfowl with pochard (630), tufted duck (240), and white-fronted geese (25). Large colony of black-headed and common gulls with some terns on island. Also lapwing, teal, snipe and probably dunlin nest there and around lough. Shore with some Mediterranean heath, _Erica erigena_.
26. Creevagh Head G 180 410 4 ha	Exposed rock	Ecological (B,O) Geological	Important seabird breeding colony notable for guillemot (750), kittiwake (940 prs) and fulmar (80 prs). Used for annual census of seabird populations; numbers currently increasing. Good exposures of Carboniferous limestone and sandstone are present and they show many sedimentary structures.
27. Coolbarren Lough L 980 860 8 ha	Fen	Ecological	A site of ecological interest with floating fen and incipient raised bog in an enclosed basin. Some water birds occur with many insects, especially dragonflies.
28. Croaghmoyle M 10 98 2 ha	-	Geological	Exposures of the faulted contact between coarse basal Carboniferous conglomerate and Old Red Sandstone occur on this mountain. At another locality, fossil plant remains are abundant.
29. Croaghpatrick L 90 80 120 ha	Exposed rock Heath	Ecological (B,Z)	Fairly rich arctic-alpine plant communities are found on the precipitous north side. There is also an old record for the mountain ringlet butterfly, _Erebia epiphron_; one of only 3 sites in Ireland.
30. Cuilkillew wood G 16 08 27 ha	Woodland (d)	Ecological	A birchwood of large size by Irish standards, relatively even-aged except for some old trees. This is a community type which is rarely well-developed.
31. Curraun plateau L 77 96 890 ha	Blanket bog Heath	Ecological (B)	High level heath with juniper, _Juniperus_ and bearberry, _Arctostaphylos_, on well-drained sites, unusual for Ireland. Very flat summit bog, important for breeding birds.
32. Downpatrick Head G 12 42 23 ha	Exposed rock	Ecological (O) Geomorphological Geological	Sheer seacliffs in fossiliferous Carboniferous rocks with horizontal rock ledges, caves, and blow-holes. Doonbrista is a classical sea stack just offshore. The area is an important seabird breeding colony, especially for kittiwake (770 prs), and guillemot (600). Ringed plover, rock dove and chough also breed on and above cliffs. Easily accessible and visible site, used for annual census of seabird populations.

Name of Area	Habitat	Interest	Description
MAYO			
Regional Importance			
33. Finny School M 028 585 0.1 ha	–	Geological	A Silurian fossil locality with a rich shelly fauna.
34. Glenisland River M 088 965 0.5 km section	–	Geological	The only outcrop of the Middle-Lower Devonian unconformity in the general area occurs in this river valley.
35. Inishturk L 61 74 500 ha	Exposed rock Heath Grassland (s)	Ecological (B,O)	A rocky island composed of Silurian slate and rising to 190m, Inishturk has a good development of heath and plantain-sward vegetation. The flora is relatively diverse and includes the rock rose, _Tuberaria guttata_, at its northern limit of distribution. Seabird breeding colonies occur on the west side with fulmar (775 prs), also razorbill (170), guillemot (200), puffin (130) and black guillemot (28 prs).
36. Kilcummin Head G 20 37 82 ha	Grassland	Ecological (B,O) Geological	The area includes a coastal section of Carboniferous rocks with some trace fossils. There are fine Quaternary features also. Above the cliffs a puffin colony (250 prs) exists, large for a mainland site, and there are kittiwake (185 prs), and fulmar (32 prs) nesting on the cliffs themselves. A herb-rich grassland has developed on windblown sand with much (15 ha) dodder, _Cuscuta_, and a varied insect fauna.
37. King's Hill G 14 02 14 ha	–	Geological	Cliff sections exposing the unconformity between the Carboniferous and Devonian periods occur here with an interesting variation in conglomerates.
38. Kinlooey Lough M 03 81 65 ha	Marsh Woodland (d)	Ecological	Ash/hazel wood with some oak and a good variety of butterflies and birds. An interesting woodland structure is developing, without recent human interference. Complex drainage in surrounding area with sinkholes, flushes, etc. The lough itself is alkaline but lies partly on peat. It was the subject of a fertilisation experiment in the past.
39. Lackan saltmarsh G 18 35 100 ha	Saltmarsh Marsh (s)	Ecological (B,O)	Large saltmarsh with grazed and ungrazed areas and clear zonation of plant types. Diverse insect communities. Golden plover (2,000), lapwing (400) and wigeon (60) are present in winter.
40. Moy Estuary G 25 25 130 ha	Sand dunes Mudflats	Ecological (O)	Intertidal feeding and roosting area for shorebirds including wigeon (270), and 4,400 waders, mostly dunlin. The mudflats behind Bartragh Island and at the southern corner are most important. Interesting plant species also occur here and in nearby saltmarshes.

MAYO

Regional Importance

41. Mulrany L 81 96 84 ha	Heath	Ecological (B)	Birch wood leading down into a sheltered stand of Mediterranean heath, _Erica erigena_ (a species found only in Galway and Mayo), with some of the largest individual plants recorded. Diverse bird fauna in woodland.
42. Port-Glenloss Point G 02 41 1 km section	-	Geological	A coastal exposure of the unconformity between the ancient Dalradian rocks and the basal Carboniferous sandstones occurs in the northern part of the area. To the south a shelly Quaternary till occurs in a stream valley showing landward movement of ice from the sea.
43. Ross Strand G 221 324 1 ha	-	Geological	A Tertiary intrusion of gabbro into Carboniferous sandstone is visible here.
44. Shangort M 110 732 3 ha	-	Geological	The Old Ordovician landscape of limestone pavement is visible here along the Ordovician/Carboniferous uncomformity. A neptunian dyke also occurs. It is an accessible site, valuable for education.
45. Sheefry Hills L 86 70 650 ha	Exposed rock	Ecological (B)	Scattered, high-level communities on shaley cliffs. Interesting flora with some uncommon plant species.
46. Stella Maris G 095 405 1 km section	-	Geological	A coastal exposure of marine sandstones and siltstones overlain by fossilferous limestone. Ripple marks and other sedimentary structures are easily seen. The site has good educational value.

Local Importance

47. Ardogommon wood M 015 840 9 ha	Woodland (d)	Ecological	A fairly rich ground flora occurs in this birch/oak wood. It is generally undisturbed and has the characteristic birds and animals.
48. Ballynew outcrop M 170 920 0.5 km section	-	Geological	A good example of the Castlebar River limestone.
49. Benwee Head F 81 44 52 ha	Exposed rock Heath	Geological Ecological (B,O)	Fine sea cliffs of quartzite occur around the Head. The strong maritime influence on the cliff top plant communities produces certain features of ecological interest. The cliffs below were the first nesting site of fulmars in Ireland (1911); now 650 prs are found with puffin (250), kittiwake (185 prs) and a few gulls.

Name of Area	Habitat	Interest	Description

MAYO

Local Importance

Name of Area	Habitat	Interest	Description
50. Carrowmore Lough shore M 22 88 23 ha	Marsh	Ecological	A deep marly lake in east Mayo with a margin of cutover bog, limestone outcrop and fen, sometimes inundated. Interesting plant communities and a few bird species occur.
51. Cloonagh Lough G 20 21 53 ha	Lake	Ecological	Highly eutrophic shallow lake with abundant insect life and some wintering wildfowl. Bottom conditions muddy rather than stony.
52. Derrycraff M 019 728 1 km section	-	Geological	Small river exposure, one of the few in existence of the Erriff Valley Carboniferous showing the transition from the Lower Carboniferous conglomerates and breccias to the more widespread carbonates.
53. Drumleen Lough G 060 095 2 ha	Grassland	Ecological (B)	Only known site for whorled caraway, Carum verticillatum, between Donegal and Kerry.
54. Inishkeeragh F 60 30 19 ha	Exposed rock	Ecological (O)	A seabird breeding colony, important for cormorants (90 prs) and storm petrel (100 prs). Barnacle geese (100) also feed here in winter.
55. Killala esker G 21 29 78 ha	Woodland (d) Lake	Ecological (Z) Geomorphological	A herb-rich woodland with good birdlife occurs on this esker, one of the most westerly of the group. An adjacent lake, Lough Meelick, is the only known site for the introduced fish, Liza ramode, in Ireland.
56. Knappagh woods L 96 80 34 ha	Woodland (d)	Ecological	Scattered birchwoods with willow and some oaks, now spreading and consolidating. The ground flora is varied and undergoing successional changes while insect life is also rich.
57. Lough Akeel quarry M 662 928 1 ha	-	Geological	An unused quarry cut into oolitic limestone and conglomerate, rocks with some lithological interest.
58. Lough Alick G 21 14 41 ha	Marsh	Ecological (B)	Calcareous lake with some marl deposition. Interesting flora and fauna, including five different orchid species; also nesting gulls.
59. Lough Cahasy L 75 78 100 ha	Grassland Marsh(s)	Ecological (O)	Interesting coastal wetland, lagoonal in origin, with large numbers of waders and wildfowl from autumn to spring.

Name of Area	Habitat	Interest	Description

MAYO

Local importance

Name of Area	Habitat	Interest	Description
60. Lough Corrib shore M 19 51 95 ha	Grassland	Ecological (B)	Eastern lakeshore areas of limestone with herb-rich communities of scrub and grassland. The characteristic calcicole flora is here augmented by the cinquefoil, <u>Potentialla fruticosa</u>, at its north-eastern limit of distribution.
61. Lough Glenawough L 99 68 73 ha	Lake	Ecological(Z)	Mountain corrie lake with surrounding cliffs. The acid, oligotrophic conditions favour char, and probably other glacial relicts.
62. Mayfield Loughs M 33 74 32 ha	Marsh	Ecological	Eutrophic loughs below Claremorris with clayey marshes at edge leading to a vigorous growth of marsh plants. This is especially so in the lower lake which is enriched by sewage. Varied birds and coarse fish occur.
63. Mocorrha lake M 22 54 29 ha	Fen	Ecological	Calcareous lake surrounded by large expanses of fen communities dominated by the sedges <u>Cladium</u> and <u>Schoenus</u>. Largest stand of <u>Cladium</u> in the county and one of the largest in the west of Ireland.
64. Mulrany saltmarsh L 82 95 22 ha	Saltmarsh	Ecological	Sheltered and heavily grazed saltmarsh with intricate drainage patterns. One of the largest in Clew Bay, and useful for education. Feeding and roosting site for small numbers of waders.
65. Owenduff at Lagduff Lodge F 820 140 5 ha	Grassland	Ecological (B)	Interesting vegetation in the river bed, flooded in winter. The flora includes ivy-leaved bellflower, <u>Wahlenbergia</u>, growing far from its general range in Ireland.
66. Porturlin cliffs F 90 42- F 85 42 6.5 km section	Exposed rock Heath	Ecological (B,O)	Important seabird colonies occur throughout this area with the largest concentration of fulmar (1,400 prs) in the county: also kittiwake (250 prs) and puffin (150 prs). An aberrant form of heather, resembling <u>Erica mackaiana</u>, grows on the cliff-top.
67. Ringarraun M 155 830 0.5 ha	-	Geological	An interesting exposure of the top of the Carboniferous limestone.
68. Robe River bog M 24 66 78 ha	Raised bog Fen	Ecological	Raised bog, mostly cutover, with peat banks and calcareous and acid pools. Interesting vegetation and birdlife. The occurrence here of the sedge, <u>Carex distans</u>, which is generally a maritime species, is of interest.
69. Rockfleet Bay L 915 950 2 ha	-	Geological	The best and most accessible section of the marine Carboniferous limestones in Clew Bay occurs here in the inter-tidal zone.

Name of Area	Habitat	Interest	Description

MAYO

Local importance

	Name of Area	Habitat	Interest	Description
70.	Rossmoney inlet L 945 870 4 ha	Marsh(s)	Ecological (B)	An artificial marsh with ecological interest derived from the juxtaposition of calcareous and saline conditions.
71.	Stags of Broadhaven F 840 480 2 ha	Exposed rock	Ecological(O)	Inaccessible and, therefore, little-known rocky islands with large colonies of breeding sea-birds. These include fulmar (200 prs), numerous storm petrels and possibly the rare Leach's petrel.
72.	Tawnagh More G 224 070 0.5 km section	-	Geological	Easily accessible exposure of the major Ox mountain fault between Pre-Cambrian metamorphics and Carboniferous breccias.
73.	Teevmore channel L 97 92 14 ha	Marsh(s)	Ecological	The site includes a narrow tidal bay and a small lake surrounded by fen. There is ecological interest in the salt/freshwater transition in an area with few other salt-marshes. Feeding and roosting site for waders.

Name of Area	Habitat	Interest	Description

MEATH

International Importance

1. Ballinrig N 82 50 14 ha	–	Geomorphological	The most interesting section of the Galtrim moraine and feeding eskers between Dangan and the Bull Ring. It is the best example of an ice-contact delta and feeding eskers in Ireland.

National Importance

2. Galtrim moraine and esker N 86 52 30 ha	–	Geomorphological	Point of contact where the Trim esker meets and crosses the Galtrim moraine. An example of an esker crossing a moraine, unique in Ireland.
3. Grangegeeth quarries N 955 794 1 ha	–	Geological	Several disused limestone quarries with a rich, well-documented fossil fauna. Type locality for several species of brachiopod.
4. Lough Shesk N 62 68 300 ha	Lake Fen Marsh	Ecological (B)	An area which, before recent drainage, had an exceptionally interesting variety of aquatic habitats including fen, some of it in transition to raised bog. Many unusual plant species occur such as the wintergreen, Pyrola rotundifolia. Although now drying out to some extent the site retains much of its interest for the time being.
5. Rossnaree riverbank O 001 717 1 ha	Grassland	Ecological (B)	A single field beside the Boyne, which often floods in winter, with a colony of the rush, Juncus compressus, found in 1968. Observation in future is required to determine whether it is native here or introduced.
6. Slane brick quarry N 953 767 1 ha	–	Geological	This quarry at Mullaghdillan is currently in use. It contains a series of light grey and brown shales with abundant and varied fossils. It is the type locality for a trilobite species.

Regional Importance

7. Altmush Stream N 790 872 2 ha	–	Geological	The stream has cut a good exposure of an unbroken succession from Upper Carboniferous limestone facies through the Namurian.
8. Ardagh N 82 95 400 ha	–	Geological	An exhumed pre-Namurian topography of semi-karst type, partially overlaid by the Namurian shales. Two important stream sections also occur in the area, one being complementary to the preceding site.
9. Ben Head O 176 686 1 ha	–	Geological	Low morainic ridge, visible in cross-section at the coast. It represents a readvance of the ice-margin.
10. Boyne Estuary O 14 77 90 ha (also in Louth)	Mudflats	Ecological (O)	An area of saltmarsh and inter-tidal mud-flats where all three species of eelgrass, Zostera, occur. Large numbers of wildfowl and waders use the area in autumn and winter. Regular peaks are mallard (200), wigeon (230), oystercatcher (580), curlew (580), redshank (420), and dunlin (3,000).
11. Corstown Loughs N 89 91 45 ha	Marsh Woodland (d)	Ecological (B)	A site of high habitat diversity with with two extremely calcareous lakes, a raised bog and an area of thick, damp woodland dominated by alder, birch and willows. Several interesting marsh plants are found.

Name of Area	Habitat	Interest	Description

Regional Importance

Name of Area	Habitat	Interest	Description
12. Crewbane N 99 94 30 ha	Marsh	Ecological	An attractive and unusual woodland of elder and blackthorn, with interesting marsh communities near the river. Abundance of the money spiders, Linyphiidae, has been noted in autumn.
13. Cruicerath quarry O 046 717 0.5 ha	-	Geological	Small Upper Visean limestone knoll with unusual carbonate breccias and rich fossil fauna, including corals, brachiopods, goniatites and crinoids.
14. Doolystown Bog N 75 51 37 ha	Raised bog	Ecological	A remnant of a raised bog, part of which shows a very well-developed hummock and hollow structure, and appears to be in active growth. This is most unusual in the county today where most of the bogs have suffered from drainage.
15. Kellystown N 864 952 150 ha	-	Geological	Rare exposure of brucite marble.
16. Lough Doo N 50 74 15 ha	Lake Fen	Ecological	Three or four small lakes occur in this valley, the uppermost being highly calcareous and covered by marl. It has little aquatic and marginal vegetation and contrasts with the lower lakes which are surrounded by a dense swamp of the sedge, Cladium.
17. Mornington dunes O 15 75 55 ha	Sand dunes	Ecological	A good variety of habitats occurs in this area, including both fixed dunes and dune slacks. The plant and animal communities are relatively rich and contain several interesting species. Wild clary, Salvia horminoides, occurs at its northern limit while the Mediterranean snail, Theba pisana, is here in the centre of its small Irish range.
18. Naul O 135 613 2 ha	Exposed rock	Ecological (B) Geological	A good Carboniferous section occurs in this meltwater channel which also has an unusual fern flora.
19. Newtown area N 91 86 11,400 ha	-	Geomorphological Ecological	Series of hills and marshy depressions representing the margin of a drumlin belt which terminates to the south at the Kells moraine. Mentrim Lough is the site of the marsh fern, Thelypteris palustris.
20. Rathmoylan esker N 79 49 20 ha	Woodland (d)	Ecological	One of the few wooded eskers in the country, with well-grown hazel, ash and some oak on it. There are also areas of the more typical hazel scrub and some calcareous grassland.
21. Stackallan river N 921 715 0.5 ha	Marsh	Ecological (B)	A rare grass, Poa palustris, grows on marshy ground by the river, one of its few localities in the country.
22. Thomastown Bog O 01 69 35 ha	Raised bog	Ecological	A small raised bog west of Duleek which is completely surrounded by carr woodland. The variety and richness of habitats are of special interest.

Name of Area	Habitat	Interest	Description
MEATH			
Local Importance			
23. Ballyhoe Lough N 85 95 55 ha (also in Monaghan)	Lake	Ecological(O) Geological	An acid peaty lake supporting good numbers of wintering wildfowl (350) for its size. These are mainly diving duck, pochard and tufted duck. Remains of the giant Irish deer have been found around the lake especially on the central peninsula. Wooded islands and shores add to its educational value.
24. Ballynabarny fen N 687 459 2 ha	Fen	Ecological(B)	A small artificial fen with an interesting plant community. This includes several uncommon species such as the horsetail, Equisetum variegatum, in abundance.
25. Bellewstown racecourse O 09 67 30 ha	Grassland	Ecological	An area of poor acid grassland, generally unfertilized. This is a rare habitat type in County Meath.
26. Bogtown N 60 43 350 ha	Raised bog	Ecological	A large, generally dry raised bog with a stream running across and underneath part of it. Subterranean course is marked by different vegetation on surface, especially by moor grass, Molinia.
27. Cromwell's Bush fen O 102 647 10 ha	Fen	Ecological(B)	An exceptional variety of communities occurs in the fen with a large area dominated by the bulrush, Typha angustifolia. Aquatic plants include the frogbit, Hydrocharis morsus-ranae.
28. Duleek Commons O 04 69 35 ha	Marsh Fen	Ecological(B)	A mosaic of calcareous marsh, fen and poor damp pasture with the spikerush Eleocharis uniglumis, at one of its few inland stations.
29. Flemingstown woodlands N 99 66 30 ha	Woodland(d)	Ecological	Mature semi-natural woodlands, rare in county. The majority of the trees are oak but many other species have been planted. A local refuge for several flowering plants and bryophytes, and the only site of the fern, Polystichum aculeatum, in the county.
30. Girley Bog N 70 70 100 ha	Raised bog	Ecological	A well-developed but dry raised bog, which has been partly afforested.
31. Laytown dunes O 168 700 10 ha	Sand dunes	Ecological(B)	Old and therefore acidic sand dunes with an interesting flora, e.g. the meadow rue, Thalictrum minus. A valuable comparison with the nearby Mornington dunes which are calcareous.
32. Lerick Bog N 67 47 60 ha	Raised bog	Ecological	A very dry area of raised bog, partly burnt and now being recolonised. A railway line and the Royal Canal traverse the northern edge.
33. Mount Hevey bog N 63 48 190 ha	Raised bog	Ecological	A fairly wet raised bog showing some hummock and hollow development but less pronounced than Doolystown bog.
34. Newhaggard N 774 566 4 ha	Lake	Ecological	Between Kilnagrass and Newhaggard the effect of the old mill weir has produced an area rich in aquatic plants and insects, typical of still or slow-flowing water. Useful demonstration area for teaching.

Name of Area	Habitat	Interest	Description

MEATH

Local Importance

Name of Area	Habitat	Interest	Description
35. Painestown quarry N 955 700 1 ha	–	Geological	Disused quarry cut into thinly-bedded Upper Visean limestones and shales which have been folded into recumbent folds. A spectacular and easily accessible example and therefore important.
36. Rockwood cliffs N 947 735 4 ha	–	Geological	An exposure of Waulsortian mudbank limestone is found on this wooded cliff passing northwards into bedded limestone. The site is mostly accessible but the cliff rises to 25 m at the south end.
37. Roristown N 767 550 1 ha	Fen	Ecological(B)	Small fen connected to river by ditch. Several local plants occur, including the meadow-rue, Thalictrum flavum.
38. Scurlockstown N 834 566 2 ha	Grassland	Ecological(B)	The floodplain of the Boyne on its eastern side is an unusual inland station for strawberry clover, Trifolium fragiferum.
39. Slane riverbank N 963 763 1 ha	Grassland	Ecological(B)	The only other known locality of the rush, Juncus compressus, but here a recent introduction.
40. Tobermannan Bridge N 827 967 0.5 ha (also in Monaghan)	–	Geological	Just below the bridge a narrow limestone band occurs in the clay river bed. It contains exceptional numbers of fossil echinoderms.

Name of Area	Habitat	Interest	Description

MONAGHAN

National Importance

1. Carrickmacross mine and caves H 811 052 20 ha	Grassland	Geological Geomorpholog- ical Ecological(B)	A disused gypsum mine producing a good section through the Permo-Trias. On the surface limestone grassland is well-developed with several uncommon plant species, e.g. the cranesbill, <u>Geranium columbinum</u>. Five cave entrances occur within the area, some of a series of about twelve caves that occur around Carrickmacross.

Regional Importance

2. Dromore Lakes H 62 17 280 ha	Lake Woodland	Ecological(O,Z)	Narrow waterbodies (180 ha) lying amongst drumlins and surrounded by extensive coniferous woods. The lakes form a valuable wintering area for wildfowl(500) with the highest density of birds in Monaghan. A wide variety of animals and birds occur in the undisturbed conditions of the plantations.
3. Eshbrack H 550 430 1,000 ha	Blanket bog	Ecological	Blanket bog occurs above 300 m in this area on the eastern side of Slieve Beagh. It contains several small acid upland lakes.
4. Glaslough Lake H 73 42 160 ha	Lake Woodland(d)	Ecological	A calcareous lake with reedbeds and several wooded islands forming wildfowl sanctuary. A heronry and a herd of fallow deer occur in the vicinity. Deciduous woods are found at the northern end of the lake with mixed woodland elsewhere.
5. Muckno **Lake** H 84 19 360 ha	Lake	Ecological(O,Z)	A eutrophic limestone lake with moderate wildfowl numbers (500) in winter and a few small marginal fens. It is important also for breeding bird species. There is considerable interest in a water flea, <u>Bythotrephes</u>, which shows a complete gradation between two recognised species.
6. Lough Egish H 79 14 100 ha	Lake	Ecological(O)	A bleak lake surrounded by rough grassland. It is the foremost wintering area for wildfowl (700) in the county with wigeon, mallard and tufted duck predominant. The area is also used by a variety of breeding waterbirds - grebes, waders, gulls and duck, including pochard. Fish population, now altered by eutrophication, once included char.
7. Lough Fea Demesne H 84 02 40 ha	Grassland Fen	Ecological(B)	A variety of habitats occurs, including a limestone grassland rich in species with scattered rock outcrops. On the western side of the site are fine woods mainly of beech, while small wet areas are found centrally. All communities have plant species of interest in them. e.g. the brome grass, <u>Bromus erectus</u> and the sedge, <u>Carex vesicaria</u>.
8. Lough Naglack H 86 03 25 ha	Grassland	Ecological(B)	Limestone grassland, calcareous marsh and the lake itself are the interesting habitats and they each support a rich flora. The flax, <u>Linum bienne</u>, occurs here at its northernmost Irish limit while many stoneworts, <u>Chara</u> spp. have been found in the lake.

Name of Area	Habitat	Interest	Description
MONAGHAN			
Local Importance			
9. Ballyhoe Lough N 85 95 15 ha (also in Meath)	Lake	Ecological(O) Geological	An acid peaty lake supporting, in winter, good numbers of wildfowl (350) for its size. These are predominantly diving duck, pochard and tufted. Remains of the giant Irish deer have been found around the lake.
10. Bawn Loughs H 72 11 95 ha	Lake	Ecological(O)	Lakes and scattered pockets of mixed and deciduous woodland. Lakes used by wintering wildfowl (110), mainly mallard, teal and tufted duck.
11. Black and Derrygoony Loughs H 70 12 30 ha	Lake	Ecological(B)	Reed-fringed lakes with some willow trees, Black Lake has an area of floating fen based on cinquefoil, _Potentilla palustris_, with the bulrush, _Typha angustifolia_. Roosting, feeding and nesting sites for wildfowl.
12. Carrickashedoge scrubland N 832 990 10 ha	Woodland(d)	Ecological	Small areas of limestone grassland occur with hawthorn, blackthorn, hazel and ash scrub. The scrub is developing into woodland and is ecologically interesting.
13. Creevy Lough H 830 070 10 ha	Lake	Ecological(B)	A reedless lake with different communities from other lakes in the region and several uncommon aquatic species, for example, hornwort, _Ceratophyllum_, and waterwort, _Elatine hexandra_.
14. Drumakill Lake H 868 188 6 ha	Fen	Ecological	Interesting example of zonation from aquatic vegetation to meadowland. Much of the community is a floating fen and it has a relatively rich flora.
15. Drumgole Lough H 591 193 1 ha	Lake	Ecological(B)	A lake on Silurian slates which outcrop in places around the edge. Characteristic and somewhat limited flora. A nearby quarry has some interesting aquatic communities, including the pondweed, _Potamogeton filiformis_.
16. Drumreaske Lough H 643 350 10 ha	Woodland(d)	Ecological	Calcareous lake with the saw sedge, _Cladium_, surrounded by wet, marshy ground and mixed woodland. An interesting combination of planted and natural species occurs.
17. Gibson's Lough H 686 123 5 ha	Fen	Ecological	A small lake surrounded by floating fens. Plant communities vary with degree of waterlogging and include cowbane, _Cicuta_.
18. Lough Smiley H 82 21 15 ha	Fen	Ecological	Floating fen communities, carr and pockets of raised bog around the perimeter give this lake some ecological interest.
19. Monalty Lough H 87 21 33 ha	Lake	Ecological(Z)	Designated a bird sanctuary, this lake is fringed with reeds and scattered willow bushes, providing a habitat for nesting wildfowl, mainly mute swans. A good variety of stoneworts, _Chara_ and _Nitella_, is present and many rudd and bream hybrid fish.

Name of Area	Habitat	Interest	Description

MONAGHAN

Local Importance

Name of Area	Habitat	Interest	Description
20. Priestfield Lough Rossmore Castle H 65 31 30 ha	Fen	Ecological(B)	An artificial lake with varied aquatic vegetation, including the bulrush, _Typha angustifolia_, and the spearwort, _Ranunculus lingua_.
21. Quig Lough reservoir H 63 36 15 ha	Lake	Ecological	A shallow marl lake surrounded by limestone grassland. Stands of clubrush, _Scirpus lacustris_, and the sedge, _Carex rostrata_, grow in the lake with some stonewort, _Chara_. Fauna includes mussels, _Anodonta_, and crayfish.
22. Tobermannan Bridge N 827 967 0.5 ha (also in Meath)	-	Geological	Just below the bridge a narrow limestone band occurs in the river bed. It contains an exceptional number of fossil echinoderms.
23. Ulster Canal H 63 32 8 ha	Marsh	Ecological(B)	While all of the Canal is of some ecological interest this section, between White's Bridge and Carson's Bridge, where the Conewaly river closely approaches it, has a particularly rich flora.
24. Wright's Wood H 652 323 10 ha	Woodland(d)	Ecological	A coppiced wood with goat willow, _Salix caprea_, overtopping regularly-cut ash. Both the ground vegetation and the epiphytes are well-developed.

Name of Area	Habitat	Interest	Description

OFFALY

International Importance

1. Little Brosna
River
M 98 11
600 ha
(also in Tipperary
N., Galway) — Grassland Marsh — Ecological (O) — The river flood-plain and its associated marshes form an outstanding area for wintering wildfowl and waders. Numbers fluctuate with the degree of flooding on the callows and shooting pressures but include wigeon (14,000), teal (2,200), white-fronted goose (200) and black-tailed godwit (4,000), all numbers of international importance. Large flocks of pintail (250), shoveler (540), lapwing (15,000) and golden plover (3,000) also occur at times.

2. Raheenmore
N 44 32
200 ha — Raised bog — Ecological — Or of the best examples of a raised bog in a basin situation. Some of the marginal slope is still intact and the site has a well-developed flora and fauna. About 50 ha of the bog are actively growing with a hummock and hollow topography. The flora is relatively rich and has been augmented with the rush, Scheuzeria palustris, which was transplanted from Pollagh Bog in 1959, before its exploitation. The plant has not been seen recently, however.

3. Rahugh Ridge
(Kiltober esker)
N 38 32
20 ha
(also in
Westmeath) — Woodland (d) — Ecological — The esker supports probably the most natural woodland in the country on such a site. Though formerly cleared, hazel, ash and oak now form a complete and well-grown canopy. There is also an interesting ground flora.

National Importance

4. Charleville
Wood
N 32 23
170 ha — Woodland (d) — Ecological — Large woods, predominantly of oak, with ash, elm, birch and an understorey of hazel and hawthorn. Some parts, particularly the island in the lake, have not been interferred with for 150 years, are therefore ecologically interesting. The lake itself (20 ha) is important locally for wintering wildfowl (200).

5. Croghan Hill
N 48 33
200 ha — - — Geological — An extinct volcano composed of tuffs and basaltic lava flows, interbedded with Carboniferous limestone.

6. Shannon River
Athlone - Banagher
800 ha
N 98 23

   a) Mongan's
   Bog
   N 03 30
   100 ha

(also in Galway,
Roscommon,
Westmeath) — Grassland / Raised bog — Ecological (O) — A wintering site and migration route of major importance to birds. The wildfowl population includes wigeon (1,000), mallard (600), teal (600), wild swan (300), and white-fronted goose (100).   The geese regularly roost on Mongan's Bog, a well-developed raised bog near Clonmacnoise.   The bog is a discrete unit bordered by an esker - the Pilgrim's Road - on the north side. It is very wet and regenerating well.

Name of Area	Habitat	Interest	Description

OFFALY

Regional Importance

Name of Area	Habitat	Interest	Description
7. Annaghmore Lough N 30 15 320 ha (also in Laois)	Lake Marsh	Ecological	Partially drained lake with a flora which is part calcicole and part calcifuge. The marginal areas show various stages of succession from open water to dry land. There is also a small birch wood and an extensive raised bog nearby. Important local feeding habitat for waders and other birds.
8. Ballyduff esker N 28 27 34 ha	Woodland (d)	Geomorphological Ecological	Good example of an esker ridge with educational potential. The plant associations on Trumpet Hill are of importance and include hazel scrub.
9. Cloghan Demesne M 97 12 200 ha	Woodland (d)	Ecological	The site consists of mixed deciduous woodland, raised bog and aquatic communities and is extremely diverse.
10. Clonad Wood N 32 19 152 ha	Woodland (d) Grassland	Ecological	A semi-natural oak woodland and with some planted beech and conifers. There is a rich fungus flora, and a varied ground flora. Nearby damp meadows contain some interesting plant species in another habitat type.
11. Clorhane M 99 28 146 ha	Exposed rock Grassland Fen	Geomorphological Ecological (B)	This is the most extensive area of limestone pavement in the county and one of relatively few east of the Shannon. It is colonised largely by hazel scrub but open areas of rock and grassland still exist. The grassland is very species-rich. The southern part of the area is a peatland with a variation from acid to alkaline peat of some ecological interest. The saw sedge, Cladium, is found growing in shallow peat.
12. Fin Lough N 03 29 100 ha	Lake	Ecological	A lake which lies between an esker ridge and raised bog and so has a diversity of aquatic and semi-aquatic habitats. Wintering wildfowl inlcude teal (80) and whooper swans.
13. Kilcormac esker N 26 21 70 ha	Grassland	Geomorphological Ecological	Part of a well-developed esker ridge with a variety of habitats from calcareous grassland to woodland of hazel and sometimes beech.
14. Lough Coura N 09 13 156 ha	Fen	Ecological (B)	A dry fen, the development of which has been well-documented from the time it was a swamp. Characteristic plants include the sedges, Carex dioica and C. limosa and the orchid, Dactylorhiza traunsteineri.
15. Lough Nanag esker N 00 28 34 ha	Grassland	Ecological (B)	Calcareous grassland is particularly well-developed on the eskers west of the lake and is notable for the occurrence of the orchid, Neotinea. The lake itself is completely surrounded by peatland and there is an interesting transition from it to the glacial drift.
16. Mount Saint Joseph woods S 08 90 38 ha	Woodland (d)	Ecological	Mature deciduous woodlands mainly of oak, occur on esker ridges along the Little Brosna River. They have an interesting species composition, especially in the ground flora.

Name of Area	Habitat	Interest	Description
OFFALY			
Regional Importance			
17. Pallas Lough N 27 19 70 ha	Lake	Ecological (B)	Limestone lake stocked with brown and rain-bow trout. Marginal marsh and grassland with a rich flora. One of few areas of open water in the county, used by up to 190 duck (mainly teal) in winter.
18. Roscrea Bog S 16 90 27 ha	Fen	Ecological	Calcareous marsh surrounded by meadowland providing a diversity of habitats. Two rare molluscs, <u>Vertigo geyeri</u> and <u>Agriolimax laevis</u>, and many other species have been recorded.
19. Slieve Bloom N 25 02 1750 ha	Blanket bog	Ecological	Extensive blanket bog is found above 390 m and it has a characteristic flora and fauna. The best area is on the plateau above the Camcor River.
20. Woodville N 07 07 105 ha	Woodland (d)	Ecological	Dense hazel and oak woodland with some conifer plantations. A drying-up lake with reeds and semi-aquatic vegetation is included. It supports some wildfowl and large numbers of snipe. Diverse ecology in different tree communities. Mature mixed woodland of oak and beech occurs at Knockydown and offers a valuable contrast.
21. Woodfield Bog N 25 36 200 ha	Raised bog	Ecological	A small area of raised bog with several different plant communities. The flora includes the clubmoss, <u>Lepidotis</u>.
Local Importance			
22. Ballintemple S 01 84 40 ha	Raised bog	Ecological (B)	An area of cutover bog recolonised by some interesting plant communities.
23. Ballycumber Bog N 16 39 160 ha	Raised bog	Ecological	A large raised bog, extensively cut on the south-east side. Plant species include carnation sedge, <u>Carex panicea</u>, a species characteristic of more western regions.
24. Camcor wood N 22 04 10 ha	Woodland (d)	Ecological	A well-developed alder wood occurs at this point in the Camcor valley above Kinnitty. Though small in extent, the community is characteristic and fairly rich in species.
25. Clonfinlough esker N 55 27 82 ha	Grassland	Ecological	Species-rich turf on an esker, with some uncommon plants. The variety of habitats along the whole esker is of value for education.
26. The Derries N 10 06 20 ha	Raised bog	Ecological	A wet raised bog to the north-east of Birr with some scattered Scot's pine and pockets of birch scrub. The area is surrounded by conifer plantations but retains much of educational value.

Name of Area	Habitat	Interest	Description
OFFALY			
Local Importance			
27. Derrykeel meadows N 16 04 20 ha	Fen	Ecological	Wet calcareous meadows on the site of a cut-over bog have an interesting flora with the rush, <u>Juncus subnodulosus.</u>
28. Esker Bridge N 55 27 15 ha	Grassland	Ecological Geomorphological	A well-developed flora occurs here on eskers that have been partly modified by excavation and agriculture.
29. Golden Grove S 12 9? 21 ha	Woodland (d)	Ecological	A planted beechwood with belts of firs, bordered by more natural woodland of alder, oak and ash. Several large, old trees and some fallen timber add to the ecological value.
30. Grand Canal N 525 311 to N 579 326 5 km section	River	Ecological	Open water and banks of the canal provide a refuge for local aquatic flora and fauna. On this stretch the canal passes through pastureland and raised bog.
31. Knockbarron Wood N 18 07 32 ha	Woodland (d)	Ecological	A planted deciduous woodland of sycamore with patches of hazel, ash and other species. Sycamore is not often used in pure stand and the area has ecological interest for this reason. Associated fauna is relatively plentiful.
32. Lough Boora N 16 18 6 ha	-	Geological	Site of an early Post-glacial lakeshore which has been exposed by the drainage and excavation associated with turf-cutting.
33. Lough Roe Bog N 25 30 665 ha	Raised bog	Ecological	A very good example of a wet raised bog, still in active growth.
34. Raheen Lough N 46 18 25 ha	Lake	Ecological (O)	A fairly shallow lake with a stony bottom. Important habitat for wintering wildfowl, mainly duck and whooper swans. Few other areas of open water occur in the county.
35. Ross & Glenns eskers N 06 08 25 ha	Grassland	Ecological Geomorphological	An interesting and rich mixture of calcicole plant species occurs on these eskers, including such plants as the burnet rose, <u>Rosa pimpinellifolia</u>, and golden rod, <u>Solidago</u>, in a turf of low growing grasses. Hazel scrub appears to the west as Ross Wood.

Name of Area	Habitat	Interest	Description
ROSCOMMON			
International Importance			
1. St. John's Wood M 99 56 150 ha	Woodland (d)	Ecological (B)	The largest and least managed woodland in the midlands. It is formed of oak and hazel with some ash on thin limestone soils. The ground flora contains many interesting species of higher plants and bryophytes, while the fauna includes species characteristic of old woodland. The area is on the shores of Lough Ree (see below)
National Importance			
2. Caher Bog M 56 84 200 ha	Raised bog Marsh	Ecological	One of the best western or transitional type of raised bogs in the country, occuring at the headwaters of the Suck River. The river itself and its associated marshes add to the importance of the area.
3. Hughestown Wood G 90 01 12 ha	Woodland (d)	Ecological (B)	The best example of an oak wood (<u>Quercus robur</u>) in the county, on a wet, clayey soil with some ash, birch, wych elm, alder and hazel. Interesting because of the absense of introduced plant species. The ground flora and shrub layer contain several species of interest.
4. Lough Fun-shinagh M 93 51 250 ha	Lake	Ecological (O)	A fluctuating lake in a fairly deep basin which has some of the features of a turlough. It has a diverse aquatic flora including large beds of clubrush, <u>Scirpus lacustris,</u> and is important for breeding and wintering wildfowl and waders, with maximum counts of over 100 duck (mostly mallard) and 125 white-fronted geese.
5. Lough Ree N 01 53 4,580 ha (also in Longford Westmeath)	Lake	Ecological (O,Z)	The second largest Midland lake and probably the one least affected by eutrophication. There are many sites of interest on its islands and shores, including St. John's Wood (see above). The lake itself has a distinct fauna with the fish, pollan, at one of its two Irish sites. There is also an abundance of the glacial relict shrimp, <u>Mysis relicta</u>. High numbers of wildfowl (3,700) sometimes occur in winter but the regular population is not well-known.
a) Bally Bay (Regional) N 00 47 180 ha	Marsh Fen	Ecological (O,B)	Much interesting vegetation occurs in Bally Bay with extensive beds of sedges, such as <u>Carex lasiocarpa</u>, and also reedswamp. These habitats and the islands are important for breeding wildfowl.
b) Yew Point (Regional) N 00 47 130 ha	Woodland (d)	Ecological (B)	The limestone of the shore is exposed around much of the lake and at Yew Point it is covered by a dry woodland. The ground flora is species rich, including the red campion, <u>Silene dioica</u>. The lakeshore itself also has interesting species, the hawkweed, <u>Hieracium umbellatum</u> and the water germander, <u>Teucrium scordium</u>.
c) River Hind (Local) M 96 60 172 ha	Lake Woodland (d)	Ecological (O)	The river mouth is important for wintering wildfowl, mainly teal, wigeon and pochard. The Ferrinch Islands nearby provide nesting sites for many species of bird.

Name of Area	Habitat	Interest	Description

ROSCOMMON

National Importance

6. Shannon River (Athlone - Shannonbridge) N 04 42 - M 97 25 940 ha (also in Offaly, Westmeath) — **Grassland** — **Ecological (O)** — Slow, meandering river bordered by reed-beds with extensive flood meadows. Some interesting plants occur in the drains and on the river margin. It is an extremely important area for wintering wildfowl and waders with the following species usually present: Bewick's swan (350), whooper swan (500), mute swan (120), wigeon (1,680), teal (650), tufted duck (160), pochard (190), black-tailed godwit (580), lapwing (1,900) and golden plover (5,600).

7. Suck River M 84 32 1,600 ha (also in Galway)
   a) Ballyforan-Ballinasloe M 85 37 750 ha
   b) Ballinasloe-Shannonbridge M 92 24 850 ha — **Grassland** — **Ecological (O)** — The flooded callows of the River Suck are valuable feeding areas for wintering widlfowl. The northern section is one of the few inland haunts of white-fronted geese (100). Other wintering birds include exceptional numbers of wigeon (5,400), and many wild swan, both Bewick's (100) and whooper (100). The area is important also for lapwing and golden plover (7,000).
   Below Ballinasloe the callows are probably less important but support additional wigeon (2,600), and wild swan (300). The river may be valuable for geese as a refuge area during bog exploitation.

Regional Importance

8. Annaghmore Lough M 90 83 200 ha — **Fen Lake** — **Ecological (B,O)** — Interesting aquatic plant communities in a calcareous lake surrounded by fen. A variety of wintering wildfowl (1,000) use the area, including wigeon, mallard and teal and there are also golden plover (2,000) and lapwing.

9. Briarfield, Castleplunket & Mullygollan M 78 77 & M 80 79 300 ha — **Turlough** — **Ecological (O)** — Three turlough areas which are generally undisturbed and important for wintering wildfowl. Teal and wigeon are the major species with mallard, pintail and shoveler. Numbers of whooper (120), and Bewick's swan (200) also occur at intervals.

10. Carrigeenroe marsh G 82 08 15 ha — **Marsh** — **Ecological (B)** — A little-grazed series of marsh communities, ranging from reedswamp to wet meadows and swamp woodland. Some quaking areas are present. The species - rich fens and lake edge communities include the sedge, *Carex elongata*, at its only station on the Shannon.

11. Castlesampson esker M 94 40 15 ha — **Grassland** — **Ecological Gemorphological** — At present the best preserved esker in the coun. Vegetation typical of dry, calcareous soils with some uncommon plant species. Interesting contrast with nearby acidic eskers.

12. Cloonloughlin & Mount Talbot callows M 82 53 180 ha (also in Galway) — **Grassland** — **Ecological (O)** — A turlough of major importance to dabbling duck occurs in this area adjacent to the Suck River. Wigeon (1,300), teal (680), shoveler (100), and pintail (75) occur in winter with waders then and on migration. Lapwing (1,000), golden plover (2,000), dunlin (300) and black-tailed godwit (800) are regular.

Name of Area	Habitat	Interest	Description
ROSCOMMON			
Regional Importance			
13. Drumman's Island, L. Key G 83 04 19 ha	Woodland (d)	Ecological (B)	A well-grown wood derived from planting in the 19th century. It consists of ash and oak, _Quercus robur_, with some introduced species. The drumlin soil is well-drained and the shrub layer and ground vegetation diverse. The site has a rich epiphyte flora for the midlands and is visited by a herd of fallow deer.
14. Knocknanool esker M 985 562 0.5 ha	Grassland	Ecological Geomorphological	A well-preserved, sinuous and slightly acidic esker with a diverse and interesting flora and a wide variety of insect species. It is easily accessible and has good educational potential.
15. Lisduff M 84 54 95 ha	Grassland	Ecological (O)	A large wintering population of wildfowl and waders uses this turlough when flooded. It includes wigeon (1,200) and, in spring, black-tailed godwit (380).
16. Lough Croan M 88 50 110 ha	Turlough Marsh	Ecological (O)	An interesting flat turlough with marsh plant communities and breeding duck in a few permanent reeded pools. Important for wintering wildfowl and waders including mallard (120), wigeon (900), lapwing (1,000), and golden plover (4,000).
17. Lough Gara M 70 95 150 ha (also in Sligo)	Lake	Ecological	The lake is important for wintering wildfowl, but they mostly occur in the northern section (Sligo). Marginal plant communities associated with raised bog support a variety of interesting species.
18. Shannon River bank N 02 43 38 ha	Marsh	Ecological (B)	Just north of Athlone and below Lough Ree the flora of the river margin is well-developed, grading into pastureland behind. The site has an exceptional abundance of the marsh pea, _Lathyrus palustris_, and other species of interest. Wet meadows provide feeding and nesting habitat for waders and other birds.
Local Importance			
19. Ardakillin Lough M 87 77 79 ha	Fen	Ecological	The lake is surrounded by fens which are rich in plant species. Used by wintering wildfowl, especially as refuge when surrounding areas dry up.
20. Ballydangan marsh M 93 33 10 ha	Fen	Ecological (B)	A calcareous marshy area at the edge of a partially cutover raised bog with interesting flora, including the orchid, _Dactylorhiza traunsteineri_.

Name of Area	Habitat	Interest	Description

ROSCOMMON

Local Importance

21. Corbally
    wetland
    M 84 80
    28 ha
    — Turlough — Ecological (O) — A turlough that is frequently flooded, this area provides wintering ground for wildfowl (200) and waders. It is beside the main road west of Strokestown and has considerable educational value therefore.

22. Corkip Lough
    M 92 43
    77 ha
    — Turlough — Ecological (B,O) — This turlough has a typical flora of grass and sedge species and includes an outlying station for water germander, Teucrium scordium, usually found only on the River Shannon. Important for breeding wader species, especially lapwing and redshank, because of lack of disturbance.

23. Cornaveagh
    esker
    M 94 27
    12 ha
    — Woodland (d) Grassland — Ecological — An unusual esker near Shannonbridge with thin oak woodland, originally planted but now assuming natural characteristics. There is a rich ground flora, particularly in a disused quarry to the south, and an abundance of passerine birds.

24. Cranberry
    Lough
    M 91 33
    11 ha
    — Fen — Ecological — A calcareous lake set at the edge of raised bog, this area contains some interesting plant communities and several unusual species, e.g., the sedges Carex dioica, C. limosa.

25. Drum Bridge
    L. Key
    G 82 03
    50 ha
    — Fen — Ecological (B) — Species-rich fen occurs as a fringe around a shallow inlet of lake, with characteristic Shannon flora and a diversity of species. They are backed by larger areas of rushes, Juncus spp., on cutaway bogs.

26. Fin & Black
    Loughs
    G 86 04
    29 ha
    — Fen — Ecological — Shallow lakes surrounded by extensive fens and marshes, supporting a variety of nesting water birds and small numbers of wintering wildfowl. A good zonation of communities occurs with an interesting aquatic flora. There is some colonisation of the fen by Sphagnum moss.

27. Hog's Island
    Lough Key
    G 830 055
    5 ha
    — Woodland (d) — Ecological — Oak- and ash-dominated woodland developing without outside influences. The area provides a safe nesting site for wildfowl and several passerine species.

28. Kilglass &
    Grange Loughs
    M 98 88
    700 ha
    — Lake — Ecological (Z) — The collecting point for fauna from three rivers, the Scranoge, Owenur and Shannon. An interesting invertebrate fauna and rich bird life occurs with some wintering swans and diving duck. The vegetation is, as yet, little known.

29. Knockaduff
    Wood
    G 886 043
    4 ha
    — Woodland (d) — Ecological — Typical hazel/ash wood with diverse flora on thin limestone soil, extending onto riverside alluvium. Rich bird and mammal habitat.

30. Lecarrow
    clay-pits
    M 985 562
    0.5 ha
    — — — Geological — Little-studied china clay deposits occur in a hollow in the local limestone.

Name of Area	Habitat	Interest	Description
ROSCOMMON			
Local Importance			
31. Lough Glinn M 63 86 150 ha	Lake	Ecological (O)	A small permanent lake in a fairly steep-sided basin with woodland or reedbeds around margin. Used by wintering wildfowl, including pochard and tufted duck (150) and wild swans (50). The island and woods provide good nesting habitat.
32. Shad Lough M 82 74 42 ha	Lake	Ecological	A shallow lake liable to flooding. It is highly productive and provides rich feeding for wintering wildfowl especially teal (300), and waders. Reedbeds and grassland have a typical flora.
33. Tawnytaskin wood G 825 050 5 ha	Woodland (d)	Ecological	A woodland beside Lough Key at an early successional stage and spreading into surrounding fields. Composed of oak, birch, ash, willow, beech, hazel and spindle with a relatively poor ground flora. Accessible and of possible use in education.

Name of Area	Habitat	Interest	Description

SLIGO

International Importance

1. Ben Bulben &
Gleniff
G 69 43
1,400 ha

| | Exposed rock
Grassland | Ecological (B)
Geological
Geomorphological | A variety of upland habitats are found in this area which supports the best-developed high-level communities in the country. They are renowned for their rich flora which includes many alpine and arctic-alpine species on the cliffs, two of which occur nowhere else in Ireland. These are the sandwort, Arenaria ciliata, and the saxifrage, S. nivalis. It is rich also in bryophytes and has a little-known but potentially interesting range of invertebrates. It is the type area for Ben Bulben shale, Glencar limestone and Dartry limestone and contains fossiliferous Carboniferous reefs. Disused barytes workings occur above Gleniff valley, where Dermot and Grania's cave is a conspicuous feature on the west side at 525 m (cf. Glenade Cliffs, Leitrim). |

2. Streedagh
Point
G 63 51
160 ha

Sand dunes — Ecological Geological

Foreshore exposures of a full section of the Carboniferous rocks of north-western Ireland occur here with fossil corals. A dune system based on a shingle ridge gives the area some ecological interest also.

National Importance

3. Abbeytown
Mine
G 665 295
2 ha

– Geological

Galena (lead) and sphalerite (zinc) ores, occurring, unusually, in lower Visean limestone

4. Belvoir and
Stony Point
G 713 328
4 ha

Woodland (d) Ecological (B)

Well-developed oak and ash woodland in sheltered position, with other species including yew, Taxus baccata, and strawberry tree, Arbutus unedo. This is the only area outside Cork and Kerry where the latter occurs. Rich ground flora, especially in clearings, with many interesting species, e.g., the black bryony, Tamus communis. Diverse bird fauna, including breeding blackcap.

5. Bonet River
wood
G 775 335
9 ha

Woodland (d) Ecological

Ash, hazel and oak woodland on limestone and alluvial soil which changes sharply in character as acid rocks appear in the west. One of the richest ground floras in the county with, for example, goldilocks, Ranunculus auricomus, and the orchids, Orchis mascula and Neottia.

6. Bricklieve
Mountains &
Keshcorran
G 70 10
3,100 ha

Exposed rock
Grassland
Woodland (d)

Ecological (B)
Geomorphological
Geological

A region of karst topography, of caves, dry valleys and limestone pavement with the mountains the high points of a plateau, intersected by parallel rifts. Fossilized coral reefs are well-exposed in the Visean limestone. Calcareous communities, especially grassland, are best developed but in places leaching has allowed an interesting calcifuge flora to appear. Scrub and woodland occur, the latter with much elm. Numerous bones of extinct animals have been found in this area.

Plate 24: The plateau of Ben Bulben with huge scree slopes, now
           grass-covered, beneath the limestone cliffs. The plant
           communities have many arctic and alpine species and
           are unequalled anywhere else in the country. Blanket
           bog covers the summit (Sligo 1).

Name of Area	Habitat	Interest	Description

SLIGO

National Importance

7. Culleenamore G 615 340 7 ha	–	Geomorphological	Raised beach with a post-glacial oyster bed on it, about 1 m thick, indicating a sea level change. One of the best examples on the west coast.
8. Cummeen Strand G 65 38 700 ha	Mudflats	Ecological (O)	Internationally important flock of brent geese (2,250) pause on mudflats to feed in October, when wigeon (2,000) are also present. About 200 geese remain through the winter, moving between Cummeen and Ballysadare Bay. The area is the richest site for waders in the county, especially for oystercatcher (700).
a) Cummeen Wood (Local) G 653 368 8 ha	Woodland (d)	Ecological	High land approaches the coast at Cummeen and a fringing woodland is developing on the steep limestone slope. Ash and hazel occur together with a rich ground flora. The site is interesting because of its inaccessibility to grazing animals.
9. Glencar Cliffs G 73 41 31 ha	Exposed rock	Ecological (B,Z) Geological	Although more eroded and not as rich in plants as the Ben Bulben area, these cliffs suport an interesting flora, including several plant species which do not occur in the former area. There is also an unusual snail species. The rock outcrops give a good section in the Carboniferous.
10. Lough Easky bog G 42 26 700 ha	Blanket bog Heath	Ecological	An undisturbed area of well-developed blanket bog occurs south of the ridge of the Ox Mountains at about 420 m.
11. Lissadell G 64 44 28 ha	Grassland	Ecological (O)	Grassland which floods in winter, with typical flora. The only regular mainland wintering area for barnacle geese (720) in the country, with numbers of wigeon and waders also.
12. Serpent Rock G 56 45 63 ha	–	Geological	A section analagous to Streedagh Point is exposed on the foreshore. The rocks contain many fossil corals.
13. Union Wood G 68 28 28 ha	Woodland (d)	Ecological	A typical western oakwood with oaks mixed with holly and rowan. The bedrock is gneiss, which produces a calcifuge ground flora with many ferns and bryophytes. Epiphytic lichens are also well-developed. This is the most important oakwood remaining in the county, though it has as yet been little investigated. It is grazed by fallow deer and is not regenerating much.

Regional Importance

14. Ardboline & Horse Island G 55 44 13 ha	Exposed rock	Ecological (O)	Low islands on the north side of Sligo Bay, these are important for breeding seabirds, particularly cormorants (100 prs on Ardboline, 80 prs on Horse Island). Barnacle geese winter in small numbers.

Plate 25

Carrowkeel Mountain, Co. Sligo, a
limestone outlier of the Ben Bulben
plateau north of Sligo. The cliffs
have an interesting flora and caves
in them have yielded the bones of
extinct animals. Pre-historic burial
mounds stand out on two of the spurs
(Sligo 6).

Plate 26: An otter, _Lutra_, a characteristic animal of many large
rivers but one that is rarely seen. The animal is
probably more frequent in Ireland than in any other
European country. However, it may suffer loss of
habitat from arterial drainage, competition from the
introduced mink, _Mustela vison_, and persecution from
fishermen.

Name of Area	Habitat	Interest	Description
SLIGO			
Regional Importance			
15. Aughris Head G 51 37 22 ha	Exposed rock	Ecological (O) Geological	A good series of Upper Carboniferous (Visean) strata is exposed on the cliffs which also form a breeding colony for seabirds. These are razorbill (20 prs), guillemot (1,000), fulmar (60 prs) and kittiwake (550 prs). It is the site of an annual census for seabird population monitoring.
16. Ballysadare Bay G 62 31 1,500 ha	Mudflats Saltmarsh	Ecological (O)	This is an intertidal habitat rich in food for a wide variety of birds. Wintering wildfowl occur, including shelduck (40), brent geese (60), teal (200), wigeon (200), and goldeneye (400). Wader flocks also use the area as part of Sligo Bay and dunlin (800), curlew (200) and bar-tailed godwit (200) may be seen. Saltmarsh occurs around much of the bay and is best developed close to Ballysadare itself.
a) Derinch Island G 60 30 100 ha	Marsh (s)	Ecological	It has been reclaimed in places, as at Derinch, where wet meadows, marshes and pools present a habitat of considerable value. A rich invertebrate fauna and some wintering wildfowl occur while the aquatic vegetation is also interesting.
17. Carrowmore caves G 84 20	-	Geomorphological	A very deep cave system occurs here, going down some 140 m. It is the deepest cave in the Republic. Polliska is a nearby pothole 129m deep, with a fine stepped profile.
18. Carrowhubbuck G 29 31 4 ha	-	Geological	A good series of Tertiary dykes occurs here on the foreshore north of Inishcrone. They show contact metamorphism in the limestone with the development of skarn mineral deposits.
19. Inishcrone spit G 26 29 84 ha	Sand dunes	Ecological (B)	An area with high eroding dunes and an extensive low-lying slack to the south of them. The flora is the richest of any dune system in the county and contains several interesting species, e.g., the mouse-ear, Cerastium semidecandrum, and adder's tongue, Ophioglossum.
20. Inishmurray G 57 54 112 ha	Grassland	Ecological (O)	A low-lying sandstone island with wet grassland and important colonies of breeding seabirds, especially arctic terns and eider ducks (200). Only four eider colonies of similar size occur in Ireland. Barnacle geese winter on the island.
21. Knockalongy & Knockachree G 52 28 200 ha	Exposed rock	Ecological (B)	Blanket bog and wet heath cover much of the area but give way to more diverse communities above the two lakes, Lough Minnaun and Lough Achree. Woodland plants grow on the cliffs here with some mountain species, e.g., beech fern, Thelypteris phegopteris, cowberry, Vaccinium vitis-idaea, and the saxifrage, S. aizoides.

Name of Area	Habitat	Interest	Description
SLIGO			
Regional Importance			
22. Knocknarea Glen G 63 34 76 ha	Woodland (d)	Ecological (B) Geomorphological	Unusually moist oceanic woodland with much ash, and a luxuriant ground flora including several interesting bryophyte species. The dry valley features and its orientation along the contours are of particular interest.
23. Lough Gara G 71 00 900 ha (also in Roscommon)	Lake Marsh	Ecological (B,O)	The northern part of the lake is an important wildfowl area and provides feeding for white-fronted goose (300), pochard (900), wigeon (600), teal (600) and mallard (260) in winter. Mute (120) and whooper swan (140) also use it in autumn and winter. The geese form one of the largest flocks outside Wexford and frequent the eastern shore and Inch Island. Several islands have nesting gulls and terns in summer. Lake level was lowered in the recent past and interesting calcicole vegetation has, in places, colonised the stony ground.
24. Mullaghmore G 59 56 35 ha	-	Geological	Deltaic sandstones and limestones featuring particularly well-displayed cross-bedding and trace fossils. Type area for Mullaghmore sandstones.
25. Strandhill dunes G 59 34 68 ha	Sand dunes	Ecological (B)	Wind-eroded sand dunes with stable and largely ungrazed, vegetated areas, contrasting with bare, moving sand. The plant species are limited but include the orchid, _Ophrys apifera_.
26. Templehouse Lake G 62 17 190 ha	Lake	Ecological (O)	A woodland of native and introduced trees, fringes the lake which is important for wintering wildfowl. Mallard (450), teal (100), wigeon (180), are usually present, sometimes with whooper swan and white-fronted geese. Numbers depend on local shooting.
Local Importance			
27. Ardtermon Fen G 588 436 7 ha	Fen	Ecological	Cut-over raised bog with both acid and calcareous plant communities in close proximity.
28. Bunduff Lough G 72 56 87 ha	Lake Marsh (s)	Ecological (B,O)	A lagoon formed by the damming of the Duff river behind sand dunes. It is fringed by reed swamp, marsh and wet grassland with a typical flora. A wide variety of wintering wildfowl occurs, including teal (200), whooper swan (40), white-fronted geese (80). Nesting habitat for duck and other water birds add to the importance of this ornithological site.
29. Colgagh Lough G 74 36 36 ha	Lake	Ecological	A limestone lake with abundant marl deposits which is unusual in this region. Typical impoverished flora but a rich invertebrate fauna, especially molluscs, beetles and leeches.

Name of Area	Habitat	Interest	Description
SLIGO			
Local Importance			
30. Deadman's Point (Rosses Pt) G 630 400 4 ha	Grassland	Ecological (B)	Several unusual plant communities, including a sward of the grass <u>Sesleria</u> and a bog rush/heather, <u>Schoenus/Calluna</u>, stand gives this site on low limestone cliffs considerable ecological interest.
31. Doonee Rock G 72 32 12 ha	Woodland (d)	Ecological (B)	A limestone bluff on the southern side of Lough Gill with steep, wooded slopes providing an interesting combination of habitats with several uncommon plant species. Lakeshore nearby has typical marsh community. Amenity and educational value.
32 Dunneill River G 435 340 3 ha	Exposed rock	Ecological (B) Geomorphological	Below Dromore West a river-cut vertical limestone gorge occurs, showing features of erosion with interesting plant communities, particularly of bryophytes.
33. Easky River G 38 36 13 ha	Marsh	Ecological	A riverside woodland of introduced tree species having a rich fauna and groud flora. Alder scrub and calcareous flushed areas maintain unusual community types. The area is of some importance locally, to bird and mammal populations.
34. Five Mile Bourne wood G 780 360 2 ha	Woodland (d)	Ecological	A hazel wood by Lough Gill at a transitional stage between scrubby grassland and mature woodland, with a rich ground flora.
35. Lough Arrow G 70 10 1,250 ha	Lake Woodland (d)	Ecological (O)	A variety of habitats used by birds are included in this area. Sheltered bays and wooded islands hold both nesting and moulting duck, particularly tufted duck, while wintering flocks on lake are mainly pochard (480), tufted duck (200) and goldeneye, with some teal. A relatively rich passerine fauna occurs in woodland on the west side.
36. Lough Na Leibe G 725 125 0.5 ha	Lake	Ecological (Z)	The only naturally spawning stock of rainbow trout on the mainland of Ireland is found in this lake. Many crayfish present also.
37. Rinn G 62 36 2 ha	-	Geomorphological	An oyster bed and raised beach similar to the one at Culleenamore.
38. Slish Wood G 742 315 6 ha	Woodland (d)	Ecological Geological	The lakeshore remnants of a fine oak woodland, now mostly planted with conifers. Tree species include aspen and whitebeam, <u>Sorbus rupicola</u>. Small areas of the ground vegetation persist, varying from strongly calcifuge to slightly calcicole in character. Serpentine occurs in the Ox Mountains metamorphic rocks at this point.
39. Yellow Strand G 57 44 20 ha	Grassland (s)	Ecological (B)	Part of the area is covered by a typical maritime grassland of fescue, <u>Festuca rubra</u>, with plantains, <u>Plantago</u> spp. The other is a machair-type (herb-rich) plant community, developed on level windblown sand. Several unusual plant species occur here.

Name of Area	Habitat	Interest	Description

TIPPERARY NR

International Importance

1. Little Brosna River M 98 11 800 ha (also in Offaly Galway)	Grassland Marsh	Ecological (O)	The river callows and associated marshes form an outstanding area for wildfowl and wading birds. In winter the most important species are wigeon (14,000), teal (22,000) and white-fronted goose (200) - all of international importance. Large flocks of pintail (250), shoveler (540), lapwing (15,000) golden plover (3,000) also occur with black-tailed godwit (4,000), especially in the spring. The geese use Redwood Bog as a roosting area. It is a fairly wet and well-developed raised bog, crossed by several eskers which also have some botanical interest.
a) Redwood Bog (National) M 9412 300 ha	Raised bog	Ecological (O,B)	

National Importance

2. Cornalack S 84 00 12 ha	Woodland (c)	Ecological (B)	A variety of limestone habitats, including dry grassland, exposed rock and an important yew/juniper wood. The flora is well-developed through lack of grazing and is particularly rich.
3. Slevoir Bay & Gortmore Pt. M 8802 M 8400 465 ha	Marsh Grassland Woodland(d)	Ecological (B)	A large bay at the head of Lough Derg, the area has extensive reedbeds with a rich associated bird fauna. The open water is also used by wintering birds. Around the edge, areas of marsh vegetation overlie the stony lakeshore and are often backed by hazel and ash woodland. The open habitats carry the characteristic Lough Derg flora: a species-rich, calcicole community of bog rush, Schoenus, hemp agrimony, Eupatorium, gipsywort, Lycopus, and the bedstraw, Galium boreale, which is here augmented by the fleabane, Inula salicina. On the south side of the bay an unusually large area of birch wood occurs on a cutover bog.

Regional Importance

4. Bellvue House R 810 950 16 ha	Woodland (d)	Ecological	Part of the Lough Derg lakeshore with a small but well-developed stand of oak, one of very few in the county. Wet calcareous grassland is found along most of the shore.
5. Cameron Island & Luska Bay R 82 91 150 ha	Marsh Grassland	Ecological	The lakeshore consists of damp grassland with limestone outcrops. Lower down this merges into marshes and reedbeds in the more sheltered situations. All these habitats have a particularly well-developed flora. A large number of duck winter in the site and there is also a variety of breeding species.
6. Derrygareen R 77 61 37 ha	Heath	Ecological (B)	An upland (225m) area of well-drained soils dominated by heathers, Erica cinerea and Calluna. The fumitory, Corydalis, occurs on some of the rock outcrops.
7. Fiagh Bog R 96 97 15 ha	Fen	Ecological (Z)	A rich fen with many molluscs, including the snail Vertigo geyeri which is found at very few sites elsewhere in Ireland.
8. Keeper Hill R 82 69 250 ha	Blanket bog	Ecological (B)	A little-studied upland region with well-developed communities of blanket bog and wet heath.

Name of Area	Habitat	Interest	Description
TIPPERARY NR			
Regional Importance			
9. Lough Ourna R 88 85 28 ha	Lake Marsh	Ecological (B,O)	A shallow lake which fluctuates in level, Lough Ourna has a moderately rich flora and supports small numbers of breeding and wintering wildfowl and waders. The marsh plant golden dock, <u>Rumex maritimus</u>, has been recorded.
10. Newchapel R 854 925 6 ha	Turlough	Ecological (B)	This site is a turlough with some permanent water and it supports good marsh communities with some interesting species. It is easily accessible and of value in education.
11. Scohoboy Bog R 97 91 160 ha	Raised bog	Ecological (B)	A wet <u>Sphanum</u> bog with a rich marginal flora, Damp woodland on the site includes bird cherry, <u>Prunus padus.</u>
12. Sheehills S 15 87 20 ha	Grassland Marsh	Ecological Geomorphological	An esker with interesting grassland and scrub communities. The adjacent raised bog gives rise to a sharp vegetational transition, which introduces some unusual species, e.g., the sedge, <u>Carex pseudocyperus.</u>
13. Templemore S 11 71 21 ha	Woodland (d)	Ecological	A variety of habitats occurs, including an interesting wet woodland of originally planted beech. This has a rich associated flora and bird life and some amenity value. An unusual hawthorn, <u>Crataegus laevigata</u>, occurs in hedges.
Local Importance			
14. Clareen Lough R 84 87 650 ha	Lake Fen	Ecological	Calcareous marsh and fen communities are well-developed in several depressions east of Lough Derg and this series of three lakes, Lough Claree, Clareen and Poulawee is fully representative of them.
15. Clare Glen R 74 59 15 ha (also in Limerick)	Woodland (d)	Ecological (B) Geological	A deep, tree-filled valley, cut in morainic material and Old Red Sandstone. The area provides a good section through these rocks as well as excellent examples of fossil ripple marks. The mixed woodland has a well-developed bryophyte and fern flora.
16. Lismacrory House R 97 99 50 ha	Turlough	Ecological (B)	A turlough with a characteristic flora including the Shannon plant, water germander, <u>Teucrium scordium</u>.

Name of Area	Habitat	Interest	Description
TIPPERARY NR			
Local Importance			
17. Lough Nahinch R 99 94 26 ha	Marsh	Ecological	Many different habitats occur with a rich diversity of plant species. Small numbers of wildfowl and waders breed and winter in the area.
18. Monaincha Bog S 18 88 1,300 ha	Raised bog	Ecological	A large and relatively undisturbed raised bog with its charactertistic flora.
19. Spring Park wetlands R 91 98 38 ha	Marsh	Ecological	Shallow lakes in limestone north of Borrisokane, representing an outlying station for the Shannon flora. They support wintering wildfowl, including whooper swan.
20. Thurles lagoon S 11 56 6 ha	Lake	Ecological (O)	An artificial, eutrophic lake at the sugar factory, of value only because of the large flocks of wildfowl it supports in winter. Dabbling duck sometimes number 1,000 and include pochard (600), while wild swan (160) also occur.
21. Willsborough esker R 89 88 11 ha	Grassland	Ecological	A good example of esker ridge community with calcareous grassland rich in species. The flora includes marjoram, Origanum, yellow wort, Blackstonia, and the grasses, Trisetum and Avenula.

Name of Area	Habitat	Interest	Description

TIPPERARY SR

Internatíonal Importance

| 1. Ballymacadam
S 076 232
0.4 ha | - | Geological | A deposit of siliceous clay of Tertiary age occurs here in a limestone hollow and contains lignite bands with a high pollen content, mainly of oak. Extremely valuable for study of botanical history. |

National Importance

2. Galtee Mount- ains R 90 24 850 ha	Exposed rock Blanket bog Heath	Ecological (B) Geomorphological	An inland mountain range reaching 905m, with diverse and interesting plant communities. These are chiefly blanket bog but on steep slopes over the corrie lakes and in well-drained sites, heath, grassland and patches of woodland persist. The cliffs above Lough Muskry and Lough Curra have mountain vegetation which includes many arctic-alpine species such as alpine meadow-rue, _Thalictrum alpinum_, the sorrel _Oxyria_, and the rock cress, _Cardaminopsis_.
3. Hollyford R 935 562 0.5 ha	-	Geological	A small roadside quarry where an outcrop of fractured Wenlockian (Silurian) rock is exposed - a rare occurrence in the country.
4. Knockastakeen Forest R 93 28 329 ha	Woodland (d)	Ecological (Z)	Scot's pine and other coniferous plantations contain the largest concentration of wood ant nests, _Formica lugubris_, in the country.

Regional Importance

5. Annacarty wetlands R 93 44 23 ha	Marsh Lake	Ecological (B)	A series of calcareous marshes and fens, strikingly different from each other though closely associated. Marl deposition occurs in some, while floating fen with some tree colonisation is seen elsewhere. The flora is particularly rich, including two bulrushes, _Typha_ spp. and the liverwort, _Riccia fluitans_. The invertebrate fauna is also well-developed. Altogether this is the most valuable wetland system in the county.
6. Ardfinnan S 085 180 4 ha	-	Geomorphological	Exposures of the south Irish end moraine in disused sand-pits.
7. Dundrum Sanctuary R 96 44 16 ha	Marsh	Ecological	Coniferous plantations surround a calcareous alder marsh and pond containing typical invertebrate fauna and flora. A few wild-fowl occur in both summer and winter.

Name of Area	Habitat	Interest	Description
TIPPERARY SR			
Regional Importance			
8. Glen of Aherlow R 90 30 71 ha	-	Geomorphological	A limestone glen, enclosed on each side by the Galtee Mountains and formerly filled by a glacial lake. Various out-flow deltas which result from the rise and fall of lake-level corresponding to the position of the ice sheet, are visible.
9. Grove Wood S 22 33 32 ha	Woodland (d)	Ecological	A young wood on sandstone near Fethard with ash, hazel, birch and some oak, and a rich ground flora and fauna. One of the few oak-woods in the county on a relatively base-rich soil.
10. Inchinsquillib Wood R 91 50 10 ha	Woodland (d)	Ecological	A naturally developing woodland with dense hazel being colonised by oak, birch and ash. The ground flora is typical of this sort of woodland with the sedges, Carex sylvatica. C. remota, wood speedwell, Veronica montana etc.
11. Killough Hill S 11 51 43 ha	Woodland (c)	Ecological (B)	A limestone hill with grassland and a hazel woodland that is evolving naturally. It is one of the few areas east of the Shannon for limestone pavement. A well-developed ground flora and invertebrate fauna occurs and the whole area has good education value.
12. Kilsheelan S 28 23 250 ha (also in Waterford)	-	Geomorphological	Terraces in the Suir valley at Kilsheelan are formed of ice-deposited gravels from the south Ireland end moraine.
13. Mitchelstown Caves R 924 168 4 km section	-	Geomorphological Ecological (Z)	An extensive limestone cave system with dry and well-decorated chambers and passages. Three separate caves are included, the Old Cave having probably the largest underground chamber of any Irish cave. The interesting and relatively well-known fauna includes the subterranean spider, Porhomma.
14. Ninemilehouse S 363 349 6 ha	-	Geomorphological	An exposure of the south Irish end moraine occurs here in a low bank.
15. Roaring Well S 065 198 1 km section	-	Geomorphological	A very large rising on the west bank of the River Suir, south of Cahir. The passages are mostly flooded and so far 720 m have been explored by diving.
16. Suir below Carrick-on-Suir S 42 21 22 ha	River (s) Marsh	Ecological (B,Z)	Low marshes and fields which are flooded at times by the river and the tide. They have a rich fauna and flora, especially of willow species. The river is an important spawning area for twaite shad, Alosa fallax, which is otherwise a marine species.
Local Importance			
17. Ardmayle pond S 053 453 2 ha	Lake	Ecological	A small lake created from an old meander of the Suir with typical still water flora and inverte-brate fauna. Such areas are rare in the county.

Name of Area	Habitat	Interest	Description
TIPPERARY SR			
Local Importance			
18. Bull's Hole S 342 396	-	Geomorphological	A semi-mature cave system close to Mullinahone It occurs in an area with much exposed limestone.
19. Cahir Park woodland S 052 235 22 ha	Woodland (d)	Ecological	Several small woods planted with oak, beech, elm, lime and chestnut and colonised by a fairly rich ground flora. The trees are well-grown and support a rich associated fauna.
20. Carrowkeale Woods R 96 51 14 ha	Woodland	Ecological	Scrub occurs in a steep-sided valley of acidic rocks with rowan, birch, willows and some oak, and patches of marshy ground. Like Knockanavar, the area forms a local reservoir for plants and animals.
21. Glenboy wood S 12 09 13 ha	Woodland (d)	Ecological	A birch wood with some mature oak, rowan and holly. The area has a typical ground flora and vertebrate fauna. Birch wood communities are rare in the county.
22. Kilcooly Abbey lake S 298 581 4 ha	Lake	Ecological	An artificial decoy lake with a varied flora, now used as a wildfowl sanctuary. One of the largest open water areas in South Tipperary.
23. Knockanavar Wood R 86 5O 16 ha	Woodland (d)	Ecological	A semi-natural woodland in a steep-sided valley with hazel, birch, rowan, oak and a luxuriant ground flora and varied fauna. Inaccessibility makes it a reservoir for plants and animals.
24. Knockroe Fox Covert S 03 39 12 ha	Woodland (d)	Ecological	The site is on the north side of a low hill (128 m) and is an undisturbed hazel wood with well-developed communities.
25. Power's Wood S 177 380 5 ha	Woodland (d)	Ecological	A small but undisturbed wood of ash and hazel with some old and decaying trees and consequently a rich invertebrate fauna.
26. Scaragh Wood S 02 25 11 ha	Woodland (d)	Ecological	Remnants of a regenerating oak woodland persist in this area of large coniferous woods and the community retains its associated ground flora.
27. Shanbally Wood R 97 15 18 ha	Woodland (d)	Ecological	A small, wet, planted wood in a predominantly cultivated area. The tree species are beech, ash, sycamore and oak. The fauna appears diverse.

Name of Area	Habitat	Interest	Description

WATERFORD

National Importance

1. Coumshingaun
   S 32 11
   260 ha

   Exposed rock
   Lake
   Heath

   Ecological (B,Z)
   Geomorphological

   An ice-cut corrie in the Comeragh Mountains including a lake, high walls of Old Red Sandstone and a fine complex of moraines. The lake is suspected of holding char. It drains through the moraine complex which carries heath vegetation. As a whole the area has a rich bryophtye flora and several uncommon plant species. It is probably the finest corrie in Ireland.

2. Dungarvan
   Harbour
   X 27 91
   1,300 ha

   Mudflats
   Shingle

   Ecological (B,O)

   Extensive intertidal mud and sand flats occur with patches of eel grass, Zostera spp. The bay is almost closed by an interesting narrow spit, the Cunigar. An important area for wintering waders and wildfowl, it has the largest wader flocks (11,000) in the county. Numbers of black-tailed godwit (1,510), grey plover (275) and knot (2,500) are particularly high, the first being of international importance.

3. Newtown
   S 704 065
   2 km section

   -

   Geological

   A complex site with an interglacial (Gortian) exposure overlain by a suite of tills and soliflucted deposits.

4. Nire Valley
   woodlands
   S 20 13 &
   S 24 14
   100 ha

   Woodland (d)

   Ecological

   A series of woodlands showing various stages in development towards the oak-dominated climax. A rich ground flora and many bryophytes occur and the site is on the eastern edge of the range of the Irish spurge, Euphorbia hyberna.

5. Portlaw woods
   S 45 15
   150 ha

   Woodland (d)

   Ecological (B)

   An important example of semi-natural, mature oak wood which is regenerating freely. The site has a well-developed ground flora with interesting bryophytes and lichens.

6. Tramore
   S 61 01
   700 ha

   Sand dunes
   Mudflats

   Ecological (B,O)

   A well-developed dune system with a varied flora and fauna of both strand and high dune communities. These include the shrubs, privet, Ligustrum, and dewberry, Rubus caesius. On the beach the bistort, Polygonum maritimum, has been found, the only site in Ireland. The back strand is an important wintering area for wildfowl, particularly for wigeon (1,500), and for waders, e.g, dunlin (1,500), grey plover (200).

7. Tramore to
   Stradbally
   coast
   X 372 966 -
   S 577 006
   24 km section

   -

   Geological

   Exposures of volcanic and intrusive rocks, intermingled with sedimentary deposits. It has an abundance of geological features and recognised educational value.

Plate 27: Coumshingaun corrie in the Comeragh Mountains, Co.
Waterford, one of a series of such hollows excavated by
a local mountain glaciation during the Ice Age. The
300 m cliffs are the home of some arctic-alpine plants.
(Waterford 1).

Plate 28

Tramore dunes, Co. Waterford,
showing a static or eroding beach
line in the foreground and actively
growing dunes at the far end.
Erosion is much in evidence in the
high dunes, with blow outs at the
back and front (Waterford 7).

Name of Area	Habitat	Interest	Description

WATERFORD

Regional Importance

8. Ardmore lead mine X 199 773 0.5 ha	–	Geological	An early lead mine, possibly dating from the 7th - 9th century.
9. Belle Lake S 66 05 46 ha	Lake Marsh	Ecological	A lowland lake with a large area of reeds at the south end and a well-developed submerged flora. Few other large areas of freshwater in south-east Ireland.
10. Bunmahon dunes X 43 99 13 ha	Sand dunes	Ecological (B)	A small area of dunes, almost removed by sand and gravel extraction, which provide conditions for the development of many distinct communities. The flora contains some species of interest.
11. Carrickavantry reservoir S 54 02 13 ha	Marsh	Ecological (B)	An artificial lake, fringed by farmland and plantations. An assemblage of mostly calcifuge plants that are rare in County Waterford and south-east Ireland occur on the west shore in the shallow water.
12. Coolfin marshes S 48 14 150 ha	Grassland	Ecological (O)	Wet fields beside the River Suir, separated by drainage ditches, are the main wintering site in Munster for greylag geese (250).
13. Danes Island X 417 977 2 ha	–	Geological	A series of Bronze Age copper mines occurs in cliffs on the island and the mainland.
14. Dunhill quarry S 507 007 0.5 ha	–	Geological	A small disused quarry exhibiting interesting graded and bedded tuffs, typical of the Ordovician volcanics.
15. Dunmore East cliffs S 69 00 5 km section	Exposed rock	Ecological (O)	An important breeding colony of kittiwake (1,400 prs), partly in harbour and easily visible.
16. Helvick Head X 31 88 1 km section	Exposed rock	Ecological (O)	High, remote cliffs important for breeding seabirds. Razorbill (110 prs), guillemot (160), kittiwake (680 prs), herring gull (160 prs) and other species nest.
17. Islandtarnsey fen S 55 01 18 ha	Fen	Ecological	A good example of the reed fens that are well-developed in this part of Ireland. Interesting assemblage of flowering plants including bog myrtle, Myrica, and the royal fern, Osmunda.
18. Kilgreany Cave X 201 940	–	Geomorphological Geological	A limestone cave in which some human remains have been found.

Name of Area	Habitat	Interest	Description
WATERFORD			
Regional Importance			
19. Kilsheelan Lake S 268 231 6 ha	Lake	Ecological (Z)	The only lake in the country known to hold breeding stocks of carp.
20. Knock ane Strand X 477 984 1.5 ha	–	Geological	Coastal rock platform showing some interesting sedimentary structures.
21. Lismore callows X 00 90 450 ha	Grassland	Ecological (O)	This part of the Blackwater valley is an important feeding area for birds when flooded in winter. Bewick's swan (100), and black-tailed godwit(1,300) occur in numbers of international importance, together with dabbling duck, especially wigeon.
22. Lismore woods R 99 00 & S 04 01 250 ha	Woodland (d)	Ecological	Well-developed birch and oak woodlands in tributary valleys of the Blackwater with typical associated plant and animal species.
23. Muggort's Bay X 29 87 30 ha	Heath	Ecological	One of the best stretches of coastal heath on the south coast with autumn gorse, Ulex gallii, and heathers, Erica cinerea and Calluna.
23. Newtown Cove X 568 993 3 ha	Woodland (d)	Geological	A coastline section exposing varied Ordovician volcanics and sediments. A small damp woodland contains the introduced annual plant species, Limnanthes douglasii.
Local Importance			
24. Annestown stream S 50 00 40 ha	Woodland (d)	Ecological	A slightly brackish marshy area above the town. A variety of communities occurs with a number of interesting plant species. A large area is dominated by willows, Salix cinerea.
25. Ballin Lough S 45 04 18 ha	Lake	Ecological	Surrounded by almost continuous reedswamp, this is a small, shallow, eutrophic lake with a rich flora and invertebrate fauna. It has some wildfowl interest also.
26. Ballyeelinan X 21 81 20 ha	Woodland (d)	Ecological	A small wood in a steep coastal valley.
27. Castlecraddock Bog S 49 02 23 ha	Fen	Ecological	An area of fen and swamp, this site is notable for the development of a stand of the sedge, Carex paniculata, which covers a large proportion of the east side.
28. Fennor Bog S 53 02 13 ha	Fen	Ecological	An interesting variety of wetland plant communities with an abundance of uncommon species, such as the St. John's wort, Hypericum elodes.
29. Glenanna X 25 81 10 ha	Woodland (d)	Ecological	A small wood in a steep coastal valley below Ballymacart, with ash, elm, elder, hawthorn, oak and sycamore. It is of general ecological interest.

Name of Area	Habitat	Interest	Description

WATERFORD

Local Importance

30. Glendine and Ardsallagh woods X 09 83 150 ha	Woodland (d)	Ecological	Mature deciduous woodland occurring above Youghal on the sandstone on both sides of the Blackwater valley. Some particularly fine stands of oak are found, with fewer conifers than surrounding areas.
31. Kilbarry Bog S 60 10 48 ha	Fen Marsh	Ecological	A large area of reedswamp and fen close to Waterford city with good educational potential.
32. Kinsalebeg X 11 79 30 ha	Saltmarsh	Ecological (O)	A roosting site for good numbers of waders (2,900) and wildfowl (900) that feed in Youghal Bay.
33. Lissaviron Bog S 49 01 23 ha	Fen	Ecological	A site close to Castlecraddock bog but having a different, more acidic flora with much bottle sedge, Carex rostrata, and bogbean, Menyanthes.
34. Sgilloge Loughs S 30 11 92 ha	Blanket bog Exposed rock	Ecological	The cliff and moorland habitats around these lakes support a well-developed, high-level bryophyte flora.
35. Stradbally woods X 35 97 71 ha	Woodland (d)	Ecological	Mixed woodland dominated by oak and beech with some conifers. One area naturally colonised, and of ecological interest.
36. Toor Wood S 292 200 9 ha	Woodland (d)	Ecological	Two small areas of deciduous woodland, surrounded by coniferous plantations, occur above Glenpatrick Bridge. One is a steeply sloping but wet, relict oakwood, the other a planted beech wood. An interesting ground flora has developed.

Name of Area	Habitat	Interest	Description

WESTMEATH

International Importance

1. Rahugh Ridge (Kiltober esker) N 39 32 31 ha (also in Offaly) — Woodland (d) — Ecological Geomorphological — This is probably the most natural woodland on an esker in the country and consists of hazel, ash, and oak with a rich variety of other species. It has been largely ungrazed and the ground flora also has some interest. The margins of the esker are particularly well-preserved.

2. Scragh Bog N 42 59 16 ha — Fen — Ecological (B) — The area is a wet floating fen, the vegetation being of sedges, <u>Carex diandra</u> and <u>C. lasiocarpa</u>, and bogbean, <u>Menyanthes</u>. Some drier mossy patches occur, raised above the general level and there is some open water also. It is ecologically a most important area, illustrating the transition from alkaline fen to acidic raised bog. It contains a large number of uncommon plants including the wintergreen, <u>Pyrola rotundifolia</u>, and the bog cotton, <u>Eriophorum gracile</u>, and also some bryophytes of interest.

National Importance

3. Carranstown Bog N 64 54 150 ha — Raised bog — Ecological — The best example of an eastern raised bog in the county with a well-developed hummock-pool complex. The flora is comparatively rich with the sedge, <u>Rhynchospora fusca</u>, and reindeer moss, <u>Cladonia rangiferina</u>.

4. Long Hill esker & Swallow Lough N 37 36 48 ha — Woodland (d) Marsh — Ecological (B) Geomorphological — Semi-natural woodland of well-grown hazel, ash and hawthorn covers this steep-sided esker. Some planted beech trees occur and are spreading. The general flora is rich with several uncommon plant species while the fauna and fungus flora are varied. The lake shore provides a clear sequence of vegetation from water to land. An accessible site, of value in education.

5. Lough Derravaragh N 40 67 1,170 ha — Lake — Ecological (O,Z) — An alkaline lake now suffering from enrichment, with brown trout and, formerly, the shrimp, <u>Mysis relicta</u>. At the west end it is bordered by raised bog and extensive flat grasslands, the result of a lowering of lake level. These and the rest of the shore have a fairly rich aquatic flora. The whole lake holds large numbers of wintering wildfowl with pochard (5,600), tufted duck (2,000), goldeneye (180), wigeon (100) and whooper swan (60). An autumn build-up of mallard (1,000) and coot (3,000) is characteristic, while many species of migrant wader occur then also.

a) Knock Eyon Crookedwood (Regional) N 46 62 70 ha — Woodland (d) — Ecological (B) — The lake runs between small but steep-sided hills at its eastern end, such as Knock Eyon and Knock Body. These consist of siliceous limestone and have several patches of hazel, birch or oak woodland on them, depending on local conditions. At Croodedwood some calcifuge species are found under oak which is unusual in Westmeath. All the sites have a rich flora, shown by the presence of such grasses as wood melick, <u>Melica</u>, millet, <u>Milium</u>, and the fescue, <u>Festuca altissima</u>.

Name of Area	Habitat	Interest	Description

WESTMEATH

National Importance

Name of Area	Habitat	Interest	Description
6. Lough Kinale Derragh Lough N39 28 30 ha (also in Longford, Cavan)	Lake	Ecological (O)	A highly productive lake with a mixture of alkaline and acidic communities round the edge. A large wildfowl population and some visiting waders occur.(See Longford for details).
7. Lough Owel N 39 57 950 ha	Lake	Ecological (O)	A rich limestone lake,important for wintering wildfowl. Counts average at shoveler (1,300), tufted duck (1,100), mallard (1,100),pochard (900) and goldeneye (80). The shoveler population is of international importance.

a) Bunbrosna
      (Regional)
      N 37 61
      24 ha
	Fen	Ecological (B)	The north-western arm of the lake has been grown over by fen vegetation which is now tending towards bog in places. The flora is very rich; it includes saw sedge, Cladium, the rush, Juncus subnodulosus, the fern, Thelypteris palustris and the wintergreen, Pyrola rotundifolia.

8. Lough Ree N 01 53 3050 ha (also in Roscommon, Longford)	Lake	Ecological (O,Z)	The second largest Midland lake and the one least affected by eutrophication. The lake has a distinct fauna with the fish, pollan, at one of its two Irish sites. There is also an abundance of the glacial relict shrimp, Mysis relicta. High numbers of wildfowl (3,700) sometimes occur in winter but the regular population is not well known.

a) Coosan Lough
      (National)
      N 05 44
      110 ha
	Lake
	Fen
	Woodland (d)
		Ecological (B,O)	Coosan Lough is bordered by large areas of reed-swamp and fen with a rich and interesting flora. It is used by wildfowl at all times of the year and the population of mallard can reach 230 in winter. In places the aquatic vegetation runs through a stony marsh to woodland. This is best developed on Coosan Point where hazel and ash occur with oak, holly and alder. Many of the most characteristic Lough Ree plants occur in this accessible site.

b) Hare Island
      (Regional)
      N 04 47
      27 ha
	Woodland (d)	Ecological (B)	This is a largely undisturbed island with much woodland on it. Both the flora and fauna are of interest.

c) Killinure
      Point
      (Regional)
      N 051 460
      4 ha
	Woodland (d)
	Exposed rock
		Ecological (B)	Woodland on the shores of the lake with a greater range of woody species than at the other sites. The steep limestone slopes are little grazed.

d) Ross Lough
      (Local)
      N 06 51
      35 ha
	Lake	Ecological	A shallow lake surrounded by fen leading to raised bog.

e) Meehan
      Wood
      (Local)
      N 03 45
      12 ha
	Woodland (d)	Ecological	Hazel scrub is well-developed here. It contains some birch and has a rich ground flora.

f) R. Inny
      mouth
      (Local)
      N 10 54
      50 ha
	Grassland	Ecological (O)	Low-lying shore with much wet grassland which is used by migrating and wintering waders,especially lapwing (5,000), and some wildfowl.

Name of Area	Habitat	Interest	Description

National Importance

9. Shannon River: Athlone-Banagher N 04 42 260 ha (also in Roscommon, Offaly, Galway)	Grassland	Ecological (O)	An important area for wintering and migratory birds. Over 10,000 waders and wildfowl use the stretch of river and its callows between Athlone and Banagher and a good proportion of some species occur in this section. Wild swans (150) and wigeon (1,500) are regularly seen.

Regional Importance

10. Aghalasty Bog N 51 69 12 ha	Fen	Ecological (B)	A small area transitional between fen and raised bog, probably based on a kettle hole. It appears that a former bog on the site has been flooded and is redeveloping. Some bryophytes of interest are found.
11. Cloonbonny Bog N 06 38 100 ha	Raised bog	Ecological	An almost intact bog south of Athlone, intermediate between eastern and western types. The area also provides refuge for migrating waders and geese on the Shannon flyway.
12. Hill of Mael & the Rock of Curry N 44 76 85 ha	Exposed rock	Ecological (B) Geological	Two hills of exposed fossiliferous limestone which has developed into pavement on their summits. They carry ecologically interesting communities with no exact parallels in the county. Grassland, which shows heathy tendancies in places, hazel scrub and cliff vegetation are all widespread. The woodland has some importance for birdlife both in summer and winter (for roosting).
13. Lough Ennell N 40 45 4,000 ha	Lake Fen	Ecological (B,O)	A large, shallow limestone lake, supporting well-researched fish stocks and a rich flora, both aquatic and terrestrial. An important wildfowl site, acting as a refuge from shooting. In winter the species include white-fronted goose (100), mute swan (150), pochard (440), tufted duck (1,230) and coot (4,650). There is a good variety of breeding birds too.
14. Lough Glore N 49 72 36 ha	Lake Marsh	Ecological (B,O,Z)	A shallow, productive lake whose water quality and fish stocks have been the subject of research. Breeding and wintering wildfowl occur in small numbers. The marshes are muddy in character with bur reed, Sparganium spp., reed-grass Phalaris, etc. The floating liverwort, Ricciocarpus, occurs.
15. Lough Iron N 35 61 59 ha	Lake Fen Grassland	Ecological (B,O)	A rich lake surrounded mostly by fen communities which are best developed at Tristernagh on the west side. Here, around some small pools, a very rich collection of sedges, Carex spp., is found along with the marsh pea, Lathyrus palustris. Fields at the southern and western sides are used by white-fronted geese (250), especially in spring. Wintering wildfowl include mallard (1,500), shoveler (500), wigeon (300), whooper swans (150), with many lapwing (2,000) golden plover (2,000), and curlew (1,000).

Name of Area	Habitat	Interest	Description

Regional Importance

16. Lough Sewdy N 22 50 45 ha	Lake Fen	Ecological (B,O)	A shallow lake with numerous islands which are used for nesting by waterbirds of at least five species. Several interesting plant species occur in the surrounding fens.

Local Importance

17. Quarry Bog & Slevin's Lough N 45 56 90 ha	Fen Woodland (d)	Ecological (B)	Semi-natural woodland with planted conifers and several deciduous species on cut-over bog. North shore of lake is a calcareous fen, rich in plant species. Interesting woodland fauna occurs also.
18. Ardan Wood N 377 342 2 ha	Woodland (d)	Ecological	Predominantly an oak woodland, planted on a steep esker slope, with mixed and varied ground communities.
19. Ballynagarbry N 18 39 19 ha	Grassland	Ecological (B) Geomorphological	An esker complex covered by grazed grassland with hawthorn scrub on the steeper slopes. It has one of the richest floras of this type of habitat in the county.
20. Derrymacegan Point N 430 810 5 ha	Fen	Ecological	A limestone peninsula on the shore of Lough Sheelin with a good example of an ungrazed fen community backed by alder/birch scrub.
21. Lough Bane N 41 77 16 ha	Lake	Ecological (O)	A small lake close to the River Inny and below Lough Kinale. It is surrounded by bog and reedbeds and used by small numbers of wintering wildfowl, particularly whooper swan (50).
22. Walshestown N 39 54 18 ha	Fen	Ecological (B)	A fen community has developed at this site on a partially cut-over bog and has an interesting vegetation. The flora is relatively rich and calcicole and calcifuge elements occur in close proximity. Plants include the orchid _Ophrys insectifera_, the sedge, _Carex diandra_, and the royal fern, _Osmunda_.
23. Waterstown Lake N 10 45 48 ha	Fen	Ecological (B)	A calcareous lake surrounded by acid bog and woodland. It has an interesting flora and fauna with several uncommon species. These include the bulrush, _Typha angustifolia_, and an abundance of the liverwort, _Marchantia_, growing on peat that is sometimes flooded. The molluscs include the mussel, _Anodonta_ sp.
24. Glen Lough N 27 66 90 ha (also in Longford)	Lake Marsh	Ecological (B,O)	A shallow lake which mostly dries out in summer. An interesting flora occurs on the muddy substrate including much bur marigold, _Bidens cernua_, for example, and also on limestone exposures. Used by dabbling duck, teal and wigeon, and white-fronted geese in winter. Also, sometimes, by whooper swan (200).
25. Royal Canal Mullingar-Ballynacarrigy N 36 53 17 km section	River	Ecological	This is one of the best stretches of an interesting linear habitat with a high density of plant and animal species. These include many Shannon species that have migrated gradually eastwards from Termonbarry.

Name of Area	Habitat	Interest	Description
WEXFORD			
International Importance			
1. Camaross Cross Roads S 88 24 20 ha	–	Geomorphological	Well-preserved and accessible fossil pingos, giving evidence of seasonal freezing and thawing during the Ice Age, similar to conditions now found near the Arctic Circle.
2. Greenville S 963 414 0.4 ha	–	Geological	The site has produced a comprehensive collection of Ordovician trilobite and brachiopod faunas and is the type locality for one trilobite species.
3. Hook Head X 72 97 800 ha	Exposed rock (s)	Ecological (B,Z) Geological	Along the low coastal cliffs is exposed a classical example of the Devonian sandstone (fluviatile) and Carboniferous limestone (marine) boundary with an abundant fossil fauna. There are also well-developed littoral communities living on the rocks at present.
4. Lady's Island Lake T 10 06 480 ha	Lake (s) Marsh Grassland	Ecological (B,O) Geomorphological	Large, shallow lake with interesting communities - aquatic, marsh and maritime. Large numbers of wildfowl (7,000) have occurred when food is abundant but 1,800 are more usual. The species are mainly wigeon, pochard and tufted duck. The islands and marshy shore are an important breeding site for terns, gulls and duck. The flora is especially well-developed at the southern and eastern ends of the area with many clover species and other annual herbs. The cottonweed, <u>Otanthus</u>, occurs on the long shingle spit which closes the lake, its main Irish station.
5. Moyne Middle S 971 423 0.3 ha	–	Geological	The type section for a particular trilobite species in Ordovician volcanic ash.
6. Wexford Slobs & Harbour T 08 24 & T 07 16 3,500 ha	Grassland Mudflats	Ecological (O)	Below Wexford the Slaney opens out into an extensive shallow estuary which dries out considerably at low tide. The seaward side is protected by Raven and Rosslare Points and behind these the North and South Slobs, totalling some 1,800 ha, have been reclaimed as areas of grassland and arable farming. Ornithologically the site forms the most important wetland in the country with 15,000 wildfowl and 26,000 waders often present in winter. Internationally important numbers of white-fronted geese (5,200), pintail (900) and Bewick's swan (200) feed on the Slobs and roost there or on sandbanks in the Harbour. Tern Island, a former tern colony, is now one such sandbank. Large numbers of brent geese (400), mallard (2,500) and teal (1,300) also occur. The waders of grassland are lapwing (4,800) and golden plover (6,800) while those that feed on the mudflats include oystercatcher (1,600), curlew (1,000), bar-tailed (800) and black-tailed (1,200) godwit and dunlin (3,000).
7. Wood village S 80 06 3 km section	–	Geological	A coastal section of a raised beach; unusual because it can be dated relative to the till above it.

Plate 29:   Part of the Wexford Slobs with the Raven peninsula in the
            distance. The flat grasslands of the slobs, which were
            reclaimed from Wexford Harbour, provide feeding and
            security for geese and duck. The photograph was taken
            before construction of a viewing hide which now allows
            close views of the geese (Wexford 6).

Plate 30:   The low cliffline on the Great Saltee, Co. Wexford, chosen
            for nesting by many guillemots, razorbills, kittiwakes
            and other seabirds. The interior of the island was
            formerly cultivated but now is reverting to grassland
            and heath with bracken, Pteridium (Wexford 14).

Name of Area	Habitat	Interest	Description
WEXFORD			
National Importance			
8. Ballyteigue & The Cull S 93 06 440 ha	Sand dunes Mudflats Saltmarsh Grassland	Ecological (B,O,Z)	This is a long **series** of dunes, with well-developed communities, occurring on a shingle spit. It is the best dune system in the county. Both the flora (higher plants and lichens) and the fauna (insects) are of ecological interest. The flora is especially rich with wild asparagus, Asparagus, dewberry, Rubus caesius and the clover, Trifolium campestre. The shallow estuary behind the dunes has been partially reclaimed but supports rich saltmarsh communities which include a glasswort, Salicornia perennis, unknown elsewhere in Ireland. Large numbers of waders (3,800), feed on the Cull from autumn to spring with golden plover (2,600), and lapwing (2,100), on the fields nearby. A small island provides a high tide roost.
9. Bannow Bay S 83 10 100 ha	Mudflats	Ecological (O)	The site contains a large area of mudflats, a saltmarsh and a sand dune system. It is important for wintering birds including brent geese (300), wigeon (800), shelduck (300), curlew (1,300), lapwing (3,500), golden plover (7,250), bar-tailed godwit (600) and dunlin (2,100). The total wader population makes it the second most valuable site in the county for this group.
10. Booley Bay S 751 057 1 km section	-	Geological	Cambrian fine-grained sediments (turbidites) with excellant sedimentary structures in places.
11. Killoughrim Forest S 89 41 61 ha	Woodland (d) Heath	Ecological	An extensive young stand of birch, oak, holly and hazel, one of the largest in the east of the country. The trees grow on a stony soil with a limited ground vegetation, except for tree seedlings. Acid heath with broom, Cytisus, and autumn gorse, Ulex gallii, occurs in the clearings. The invertebrate fauna is rich in species of butterfly and moth and other insects. Documentation on the area exists from the period 1890 - 1923 and the area as a whole is of high educational value.
12. Raven Point T 11 23 150 ha	Sand dunes Marsh	Ecological	A complex of interesting dune communities occurs in this area. They are largely ungrazed except by rabbits but have often been modified by afforestation. Damp areas are found on the site of former blowouts and have a particularly interesting flora. A rich invertebrate fauna occurs on the beach and in the dunes, including species sensitive to disturbance that have disappeared elsewhere. The site is also a feeding area for coastal migrant birds, especially passerines.
13. St. Helen's Harbour T 150 100 4.5 ha	-	Geological	A pre-Caledonian basement section exposing a complex sequence of deformation and intrusive features on a wave-cut platform.

Name of Area	Habitat	Interest	Description

WEXFORD

National Importance

14. Saltee Islands X 95 79 125 ha	Exposed rock Heath Grassland	Ecological (B,O)	Islands of Pre-Cambrian gneiss and granite having large seabird breeding colonies, much studied in recent years. Nesting population includes fulmar (300 prs), gannet (270 prs on Great Saltee), puffin (1,430), guillemot (13,000), razorbills (6,400), kittiwake (1,280 prs), cormorants (280 prs on Little Saltee) and shags (370 prs). The calcifuge vegetation has also several features of interest in its heath and maritime communities.
15. Screen Hills T 10 29 148 ha	Lake Marsh Fen Raised bog	Ecological Geomorphological	A classic kame and kettle landscape with many lake basins, marking the sites of former ice blocks, in a sandy moraine. The lakes have widely different plant and animal communities, despite very similar environmental factors. Incipient raised bog occurs at Doo Lough itself with acidic fen around many of the other ponds.

Regional Importance

16. Ballyhack S 700 100 1 ha	Grassland Heath	Ecological (B)	Interesting and particularly diverse communities of light-soil plants grow here. They include many clovers, for example, Trifolium striatum, T. ornithopodioides and T. glomeratum.
17. Ballymoney Strand T 22 60 11 ha	–	Geological Ecological (B)	Exposures of the Arenig-Caradoc unconformity in the Ordovician are found in this area, along with good examples of several rock formations widespread inland. Characteristic flora on boulder clay and rock outcrops, including the most southerly location of the ragwort, Senecio erucifolius.
18. Barrow saltmeadows S 68 17 & S 71 14 83 ha	Saltmarsh	Ecological (B)	Several areas of sheltered saltmarsh, grading into freshwater swamp. A sedge species, Carex divisa, occurs sporadically; it is extinct elsewhere in Ireland.
19. Curracloe T 11 27 4 km section	Marsh (s)	Ecological (B) Geological	A large coastal section of a moraine marking the point where the Irish Sea ice (Midlandian age) was temporarily stationary. Sand dunes, backed by marshes and lagoons, lie inland. The calcareous marsh flora includes the water parsnip, Berula, and the dock, Rumex hydrolapathum. Small numbers of ducks and waders use dune slacks and ponds in winter.
20. Kilmore Quay S 95 03 35 ha	–	Geological	Extensive intertidal exposure of the Rosslare Complex rocks, showing the latest phase in their evolution.

Name of Area	Habitat	Interest	Description

Regional Importance

21. Macmine marshes S 98 32 110 ha	Fen Marsh(s)	Ecological (B)	This area carries the most extensive and best developed reedswamp in the county. It has been little studied, but interesting aquatic plants include water starwort, Callitriche truncata, not so far found elsewhere. A diversity of wet habitats occurs with rich plant and animal communities.
22. Mountgarrett S 725 280 4 ha	Exposed rock	Ecological (B)	Just above New Ross, on the steep bank of the Barrow, a woodland of oak, ash and sycamore occurs with an acidic ground flora. The plant species saw wort, Serratula, which is recorded nowhere else in Ireland, grows close to the river on rocks that are occasionally flooded. Invertebrate and bird faunas seem relatively rich.
23. Tacumshin Lake S 05 06 470 ha	Mudflats	Ecological (B,O)	A shallow lake, formerly tidal but now brackish, with a changing flora and rich invertebrate fauna. Colonisation of the lake bed by salt-tolerant species occurs in summer. A feeding and roosting site for wildfowl and waders. Maximum counts include important numbers of brent geese (500), wigeon (800), pochard (100) and scaup (200).

Local Importance

24. Ballynabarny Wood S 995 410 8 ha	Woodland (d)	Ecological	A natural stand of secondary woodland with hazel on steep sides of a river valley. Some oak and willows grow beside the river. Well-developed ground flora and bryophytes.
25. Bunclody slate quarries S 90 54 12 ha	Heath	Ecological (B)	Fairly good example of heath, modified by quarrying. The birdsfoot, Ornithopus, is one of the more interesting plants that occur.
26. Castlebridge marsh T 04 25 95 ha	Marsh (s) Saltmarsh	Ecological (B)	Reedswamp, sedge and saltmarsh vegetation, with a good zonation related to salinity. The communities are species-rich with the flat-sedge, Blysmus, the scurvy grass, Cochlearia anglica and the strawberry clover, Trifolium fragiferum.
27. Clone Fox Covert T 00 46 15 ha	Woodland (d)	Ecological	A small but pure oakwood with flora representative of acid soils.
28. Courtown Dunes and Glen T 20 57 61 ha	Sand dunes Woodland (d)	Ecological	Old dune system, artifically planted with sea buckthorn which now gives extensive cover. Sycamore woodland on dune crest makes this one of only wooded dunes in county. The area has an interesting ground flora with ferns prominent. Just up the Owenavorragh River, which has been extensively afforested, a diverse and interesting ground flora occurs in a poplar stand. Several rare species may still survive here and the site has educational value.

Plate 31:   Fresh glacial landforms forming the Screen Hills, Co.
            Wexford.   They are part of the end moraine of the last
            ice advance which began melting about 10,000 years ago.
            The till deposits contained blocks of ice which caused
            subsidence and depressions (kettle holes) when they
            melted (Wexford 15).

Plate 32:   The Devils Glen, Co Wicklow, a mixed woodland with much
            oak and at this point Scot's pine.   The high canopy and
            clearings create a good habitat for woodland birds and
            insects (Wicklow 21).

Name of Area	Habitat	Interest	Description
WEXFORD			
Local Importance			
29. Forth Mountain S 97 18 55 ha	Heath	Ecological Geomorphological	Dry acid heath on quartzite, of considerable ecological interest as the most south-easterly heath in the country. The community is frequently subjected to burning and any peat development is thin. Tors are well-developed on the summit ridge.
30. Keeragh Islands S 86 05 17 ha	Exposed rock	Ecological (O)	Samll seabird breeding colony, with cormorant (88 prs) the most notable species.
31. Mount Leinster and Blackstairs Mountains S 83 52 60 ha	Exposed rock Blanket bog	Ecological (B)	Best developed mountain communities in the county including a few arctic alpine species and interesting vegetation above the valley of the River Urrin. Large population of grouse and other mountain birds.
32. Oaklands Wood S 71 26 26 ha	Woodland (d)	Ecological	Oakwood occurs here amongst conifers and has a characteristic ground flora and fauna. The area is close to New Ross and has educational value.
33. Rosslare sandhills T 09 6 15 ha	Grassland	Ecological (B)	Stabilized dunes tending to slight acidity with heather, _Calluna,_ occurring in a few places. Most noticeable vegetation is the naturalised tree lupin, _Lupinus arboreus,_ but the heathy grassland includes many species of interest, e.g., moonwort, _Botrychium_ and the sorrel, _Rumex tenuifolius._
34. St. Margaret's shore T 12 06 12 ha	Sand dunes Grasslands	Ecological (B)	Typical type of Wexford coastline with interesting communities. Centre of distribution for plants of sandy soils, particularly wild clary, _Salvia_ and clovers.
35. Urrin head-waters S 86 48 18 ha	Marsh	Ecological	An interesting variety of natural communities occurs in this river valley at 130 m. They include mineral flushes, incipient blanket bog and woodland of alder and oak. Characteristic plants are found, e.g., the bell-flower _Wahlenbergia_ and the butterwort, _Pinguicula lusitanica._

Name of Area	Habitat	Interest	Description

WICKLOW

International Importance

1.   **Liffey Head**
O 13 13
1,700 ha
   Blanket bog
   Ecological

An excellent example of high altitude blanket bog occurs in the saddle area between Tonduff and Kippure mountains. It has suffered marginal cutting and some burning but remains relatively intact and free from the peat erosion that affects the summits nearby. The characteristic flora is well-developed.

2.   **Slieveroe**
T 211 888
1.0 ha
   -
   Geological

A rock outcrop along a lane, containing shelly faunal facies in Ordovician volcanic ash. It forms the type locality for two particular trilobites.

National Importance

3.   **Athdown moraine**
O 07 14
200 ha
   -
   Geomorphological

The site is a moraine and its associated gravels which were produced by a local mountain glaciation. The gravels lie at a lower level than that of glacial Lake Blessington showing that they were laid down after its disappearance and therefore after the main glaciation.

4.   **Bray Head**
O 19 17
300 ha
   Heath
Exposed rock
   Ecological
Geological

A variety of habitats occurs, including well-developed heath on quartzite, and interesting herb communities on the screes and drift deposits on the seaward side. The area has a varied invertebrate fauna also, rich in Lepidoptera. Nesting seabirds are gulls, fulmar (40 prs), kittiwake (30 prs) and black guillemot (30 prs). The rock is fossiliferous Cambrian turbidite with cliff exposures of a number of sedimentological features of interest.

5.   **Brittas Bay & Buckroney**
T 29 79
200 ha
   Sand dunes
Fen
Grassland
   Ecological (B)

An extensive sand dune system with well-developed plant communities of dry and wet sand. A rich flora persists, despite heavy amenity use, and contains several interesting species, for example, the saxifrage, _S. granulata_ and the rush _Juncus acutus_, here near its northern limit of distribution. The dunes have cut off the outflow of a small river at Mizen Head and a fen, Buckroney Marsh, has developed on the site. It contains an abundance of the marsh fern, _Thelypteris palustris_.

6.   **Glendalough valley**
T 11 96
400 ha
   Lake
Woodland (d)
   Ecological (B,O,Z)
Geomorphological

A fine glaciated valley showing many characteristic features. The overdeepened lakes are separated by a delta of material brought down from a hanging valley on the south side. The lakes are oligotrophic in nature and contain a race of char. Marsh vegetation occurs sparsely except at the west end where much granite sand has been washed in from mines. The Lower Lake has a peaty shore with an interesting plant community. Heath or coniferous woods cover much of the valley sides but above the Lower Lake a well-developed oakwood occurs with a rich variety of associated organisms, particularly birds.

Name of Area	Habitat	Interest	Description

National Importance

Name of Area	Habitat	Interest	Description
7. Glen of the Downs T 26 11 95 ha	Woodland (d)	Ecological Geomorphological	Semi-natural oakwood with holly fills much of this valley which is the largest example of a glacial overflow channel in the country. The community is well-developed and especially pure on the western side. Elsewhere there are some introduced species. The ground flora is mostly of calcifuge plants with occasional patches of heath. More base-demanding herbs occur on the valley floor. The bird fauna is also of some interest and includes several unusual species. Part of the area is now a Nature Reserve.
8. Lough Bray, Upper and Lower O 13 16 90 ha	Lake Heath	Ecological (B) Geomorphological	Two of the most spectacular corries in the east of Ireland, containing acid lakes with some interesting plant species and a fine sequence of moraines. Surrounding blanket bog is mixed with heath communities. The lichen flora on trees contains species of interest.
9. Lough Ouler O 09 02 38 ha	Exposed rock Heath	Geological Ecological (B)	A variety of habitats occur, including heath, blanket bog, cliffs and the acid lake. The alpine vegetation on the cliffs is relatively rich and there are several interesting plant species. A succession of moraines is associated with the corrie while unusual rock structures occur in the high back wall.
10. Lugnaquillia & Glenmalur T 06 92 3,700 ha	Exposed rock Heath	Ecological (B,O) Geological Geomorphological	This is the centre of the Leinster granite where remnants of the schist aureole are exposed on the top of Lugnaquillia. Glenmalur is a fine glaciated trough with several hanging valleys on its sides. A variety of habitats, with a well-developed high level flora, is found. The stream invertebrates and the bird fauna are similarly interesting.
11. The Murrough T 31 02 1,700 ha	Lake Marsh (s) Fen Grassland	Ecological (B,O)	The Murrough itself is the shingle ridge that forms almost the entire coastline between Greystones and Wicklow. It has ponded the drainage water of much of the Calary plateau, creating extensive lagoonal marshes and a lake, Broad Lough (61 ha). Seaward escape of water occurs in two places only, at the Breaches and at Wicklow town and here saltmarsh is well-developed though small in extent. Elsewhere, the fresh and brackish marshes have an extremely rich and diverse flora, including many Midland species. Reedswamp, fen, calcareous grassland, low sand dunes and shingle are the other habitats represented. The flora of dry sandy soils is especially well-developed close to Wicklow town where the clovers include _Trifolium subterraneum_ and _T. scabrum_. The bird life is diverse at all seasons and about 60 species breed in the area. Winter numbers fluctuate widely with weather conditions and the degree of flooding. The area is most valuable for Bewick's swan (100), greylag goose (75) and wigeon (900) but many other species occur for short periods. Other animals have been little worked on except for the Lepidoptera but these indicate a species richness similar to the flora.

Name of Area	Habitat	Interest	Description

WICKLOW

National Importance

12. Powerscourt Waterfall O 19 11 15 ha	Exposed rock Woodland (d)	Ecological (B) Geomorphological Geological	A steep 100 m waterfall, formerly used by ice, marking a well-exposed schist/granite junction with garnetiferous fold structures. It is fringed by steeply-sloping heaths grading into open oak-wood. The moist conditions around the waterfall support extremely rich bryophyte and fern communities while many lichen species of interest are found on the trees.
13. Rathdrum rail-way cutting T 205 894 0.5 km section	-	Geological	The base of the Caradoc volcanic sequence is exposed here containing taxonomically important graptolites. Site of much past and present study.
14. Rathdrum woodlands T 18 90 250 ha	Woodland (d)	Ecological	In the valley of the Avonmore River bewteen Clara and Rathdrum, semi-natural oak woodland is extensive, though it has been cleared in places for conifer plantations. Good stands persist, however, and the community is very well-developed. There is a diversity of acid habitats differing in slope and soil thickness and the ecological value of the unit is high.
15. The Scalp O 21 20 16 ha (also in Dublin)	-	Geomorphological	The best and most accessible glacial outwash channel in the Dublin area. It is now a dry valley with block scree on both sides, covered by heath and woodland vegetation.
16. Upper Lockstown delta N 98 02 90 ha	-	Geomorphological	The last surviving glacial meltwater delta in the east of Ireland; essential to the chronology of the Dublin region.

Regional Importance

17. Arklow Rock T 24 70 15 ha	Heath	Ecological (B) Geological	Ordovician volcanic intrusion forming a knoll of rhyolite. The remaining vegetation is sandy heath with a flora typical of the south-east coast. It contains several clovers, Trifolium spp., and also the birdsfoot, Ornithopus.
18. Avoca River valley T 22 76 500 ha	Woodland (d)	Ecological (B,O)	Deciduous stands of oak occur with coniferous woodland in this area, around Woodenbridge and Glenart Castle. They have a characteristic ground flora of woodrush, Luzula sylvatica, but on deeper soils a variety of interesting species occurs. Birdlife is well-developed.
19.. Ballyman Glen O 22 18 20 ha	Fen Marsh	Ecological (B)	Calcareous marsh and fen vegetation occurs on the sloping valley side with an unusually large number of sedge species and some other interesting plants. One of only two sites in county for an orchid species.

Name of Area	Habitat	Interest	Description
WICKLOW			
Regional Importance			
20. Dargle River valley O 24 17 18 ha	Woodland (d) Exposed rock	Ecological (B) Geological	The best exposure of the Ordovician and Bray group junction in the county. Oak woodland and hazel scrub occur elsewhere with some uncommon plant species. Luxuriant mosses in river gorge.
21. Devil's Glen T 25 99 250 ha	Woodland (d)	Ecological (B,Z)	Wood in steep river gorge, dominated by oak and holly with a rich ground flora. Varied and abundant bryophytes with some uncommon species. Distinctive invertebrate fauna and interesting birds.
22. Ferrrybank T 26 74 32 ha	Sand dunes Lake	Ecological (B,O)	An eroded and much modified dune system at Arklow, still retaining typical dry and wet areas, one of which runs into a lagoonal lake at the south end. The dune flora is interesting for a horsetail, Equisetum moorei, which is a hybrid known only from the Wicklow/ Wexford coastline. Some marsh plants occur around the lake which carries wintering wildfowl,e.g., pochard and wild swans, in severe weather.
23. Glendalough mines T 09 96 175 ha	-	Geological	Typical Wicklow lead mines with small quantities of the sulphide minerals occurring along the granite/schist contact present in tip heads. Valuable site for educational use.
24. Glenmacnass O 11 02 250 ha	-	Gemorphological Geological	An overdeepened, glaciated valley with a waterfall marking the junction of the Wicklow granite and its surrounding schists. A series of moraines in the valley floor below are of particular interest in studies of local glaciations.
25. Great Sugarloaf O 24 13 750 ha	-	Geomorphological	Steep quartzite mountain which stood as a nunatak and was unmodified by ice erosion. It can be contrasted with Bray Head and Howth which were both over-ridden by ice.
26. Holdenstown Bog S 88 85 12 ha	Raised bog Fen	Ecological	Small raised bogs have developed in two kettle holes here, with a surface dominated by Sphagnum moss, cranberry, Vaccinium oxycoccus, and heather, Calluna. Areas of floating fen also occur around the edges.
27. Hollywood Glen N 93 02 50 ha	-	Geomorphological	Dry, steep-sided channel complex formed sub-marginally beneath the ice by drainage from the ice-dammed Lake Blessington. Good example of a glacial meltwater channel cut in rock.
28. Lowtown Fen S 84 92 13 ha	Fen Marsh	Ecological	A good example of ungrazed fen and reedswamp with a rich flora. This includes about nine sedges species, Carex, the grass, Catabrosa, and marsh helleborine, Epipactis palustris.

Name of Area	Habitat	Interest	Description

WICKLOW

Regional Importance

Name of Area	Habitat	Interest	Description
29. Lough Tay & Lough Dan O 16 04 & O 16 08 1200 ha	Lake Fen	Ecological (B,Z)	Interesting moraine-dammed acid lakes; Lough Dan is in an overdeepened valley and Lough Tay is a corrie. The lakes hold a race of char and probably other glacial relicts also. The flora includes an interesting stonewort. Patches of fen vegetation occur by Lough Dan but elsewhere marginal vegetation is sparse. Above the lakes woodland occurs, with a canopy predominately of oak with some birch. The calcifuge ground flora includes many bryophytes.
30. Maherabeg T 32 87 53 ha	Sand dunes	Ecological (B)	These are little damaged sand dunes with a typical flora and fauna. The vegetation includes several uncommon plant species, especially sedges, e.g., Carex muricata, C. vesicaria and an interesting hybrid.
31. The Motte Stone T 200 830 1.0 ha	-	Geomorphological	A large erratic carried from Glenmalur, by the Brittas glaciation, to the Meeting of the Waters.
32. Poulaphuca Reservoir O 00 10 3,500 ha	Lake Grassland	Ecological (O)	The only large area of open water in the county, important for wintering and some nesting wildfowl and wader species. Nationally important greylag goose population (275), in fields on south west shore. Other wintering birds include mallard (300), teal (250), wigeon (350), and smaller numbers of many other species.
33. Powerscourt woodland O 22 17 250 ha	Woodland (m)	Ecological (B,O)	The river valleys have been planted with many species of tree and the resulting woodland is rich in associated plants and animals. Some parts have natural features, especially the fringe of hazel and alder that occurs on the sandy and rocky ground around the river. Well-developed beech stands occur and have a rich fungus flora.
34. Rathdangan end moraine S 97 86 200 ha	-	Geomorphological	A glacial moraine and sandy outwash fan with a clear ice contact indicating the eastern midland limit of the last midland ice sheet. Interesting till deposits occur in the area, pitted with kettle-holes.
35. Raven's Glen O 18 14 100 ha	Exposed rock Blanket bog	Ecological Geological	The area between Maulin and Tonduff South has exposures of the granite/schist boundary, with a well-developed crush structure and folded garnetiferous beds. The riverside grassland, blanket bogs, and cliffs have a flora with interesting species of higher plants and bryophytes.

Name of Area	Habitat	Interest	Description
WICKLOW			
Regional Importance			
36. Templerainey T 25 77 750 ha	–	Geomorphological	An area of drift marking the margin of the last glacial advance from the Irish Sea. Well-formed pingos lie on other, older, drift areas nearby.
37. Toor Channel N 95 03 21 ha	–	Geomorphological	The site of a glacial spillway which was once the highest outlet of Lake Blessington.
Local Importance			
38. Askintinny T 25 69 39 ha	Sand dunes	Ecological	Stabilised and intact dunes with the characteristic flora of the south Wicklow/ Wexford coastline.
39. Ballinacor Wood T 13 89 150 ha	Woodland (d)	Ecological	Steep hillside wood with very old oak trees with some birch, and a typical ground flora of the hard fern, Blechnum, wood sorrel, Oxalis and bluebell, Hyacinthoides. Rhododendron also occurs.
40. Ballycore Rath S 81 94 10 ha	Grassland	Ecological (B)	A morainic drift deposit with steep sides is covered by calcareous grassland, rich in typical species. The flora includes salad burnet, Poterium, and yellow wort, Blackstonia.
41. Ballymoyle T 240 794 0.5 ha	–	Geological	Rhyolitic volcanic rocks are exposed showing amygdaloidal lavas.
42. Ballynamona marsh T 27 82 37 ha	Marsh	Ecological	A variety of habitats occurs from dry hills and marsh to a little open water. The range of plant communities is interesting.
43. Drumbawn-Carriagower Bog O 22 07 150 ha	Fen	Eoological	A very wet area on the Calary plateau showing a transitional stage between fen and bog. It has a rich and varied flora, including Sphagnum mosses, ragged robin, Lychnis, and the sedge, Carex curta.
44. Dunlavin marshes N 85 03 24 ha (also in Kildare)	Marsh Fen	Ecological	One of the most extensive series of marsh and fen areas in the county, with a diverse and interesting flora. Calcareous drainage water from nearby moraine allows many species, common in Kildare but rare in Wicklow, to grow.
45. Glenealy wood T 25 92 40 ha	Woodland (d)	Ecological	Small patches of deciduous woodland dominated by oak, and surrounded by conifer plantations. The ground flora is often well-developed.

Name of Area	Habitat	Interest	Description

Local Importance

Name of Area	Habitat	Interest	Description
46. Glencree O 17 16 250 ha	Woodland (d)	Ecological	Woodland on the floor of the valley is dominated by oak, with birch, hazel, aspen and a typical ground flora. Areas of blanket bog are found also.
47. Glen Ding O 16 15 11 ha (also in Kildare)	-	Geomorphological	A dry glacial valley which acted as an overflow channel into Lake Blessington.
48. Kilmacanogue marsh O 25 13 10 ha	Marsh	Ecological	A wet area with a well-developed marsh flora. The tufted sedge, _Carex paniculata_, is common, sometimes beneath alder and willow trees.
49. Knocksink Wood O 21 18 28 ha	Woodland (d)	Ecological (B)	Several remnants of mixed deciduous woodland with planted conifers occur on the banks and gorge of the Glencullen River. They contain a rich and diverse ground flora with some unusual plant species and a varied bryophyte flora, especially associated with the river itself. Some interesting insects have been recorded in the area.
50. Lemonstown marshes N 92 05 60 ha	Marsh	Ecological	Esker complex with several areas of calcicole marsh and a typical flora and invertebrate fauna. The nutrient richness of the site is shown by the liverwort, _Riccia fluitans_.
51. Lockstown Bridge N 980 032 7 ha	Heath	Ecological (B)	Wet sandy ground on granite beside the Kings River, the area has a heath flora including the mountain pansy, _Viola lutea_, rare in the east of Ireland.
52. Lough Nahanagan T 08 99 26 ha	Exposed rock	Ecological	Lake in a steep-sided corrie. The area includes a variety of habitats and a representative mountain flora. The cliffs harbour some species of interest.
53. Poulaphuca Gorge N 947 085 1 ha	Exposed rock Woodland (d)	Ecological (B)	Dry river gorge with woods dominated by beech, with laurel, sycamore and an interesting and well-developed ground flora. Community on rock includes the rock cress, _Arabis hirsuta_.
54. The Quill O 24 13 10 ha	Woodland (d)	Ecological	Secondary woodland, dominated by oak, birch and holly with a typical ground flora. Some work has been done on the invertebrate fauna.
55. Vartry Reservoir O 20 06 18 ha	Marsh	Ecological (B)	Marshy ground at the north end of the reservoir, backed by hillocks of drier ground. Lake bed mud exposed when water levels drop. An interesting association of plants occurs with some species unusual in the east of Ireland.
56. Wicklow Head T 345 924 5 ha	Heath Exposed rock	Ecological	A variety of habitats with a dry-soil flora and several rare plant species. Many species of seabirds nest on the cliffs in small numbers; those involved are fulmar, shag, great black-backed and herring gulls, razorbill and black guillemot.

6. GLOSSARY

The following notes are not strict definitions but give the sense of the terms as used in this report. The names of common rocks and of organisms are not included.

Alluvium, alluvial: fine sediment deposited by a river or the sea.

Arctic-alpine: a plant or animal found today mainly in the Alps or in the Arctic regions or in both. Cf. glacial relict.

Base, base-rich: neutral or alkaline constituents of the soil, usually calcium from limestone. Such a habitat often has a abundant mineral supply.

Breccia: a rock formed of compacted angular scree.

Brucite: a white or greenish mineral consisting of magnesium hydroxide.

Bryophyte: a moss or a liverwort (q.v.), i.e., a non-woody plant of small size that reproduces by spores.

Calcareous: rich in calcium carbonate, i.e., lime.

Calcicole: a plant usually restricted to soils with a plentiful supply of bases, e.g., calcium carbonate from shells or limestone.

Calcifuge: a plant restricted to acid soils with a very low content of bases.

Caledonian: a phase of mountain building in the lower Palaeozoic (q.

Cambrian: an early period which saw the first major life forms on the earth, 600-500 million years ago (Table 2).

Carboniferous: a period 370-280 million years ago when much limestone was laid down (Table 2).

Carr: a community of sedges and shrubs, usually willows, that may develop in an alkaline fen.

Climax: the final stable community produced by the colonisation of open ground: oak woodland or peat bog in this country.

Conglomerate: a sandstone including rounded pebbles or rocks.

Corrie: a cup-shaped depression on a mountain side excavated by ice; usually the source of a valley glacier which escapes over a low lip.

Cretaceous: a period 135-70 million years ago when chalk was
    mainly deposited (Table 2).

Dalradian: ancient metamorphic rocks of Pre-Cambrian or Lower
    Palaeozoic age (Table 2).

Devonian: a period 415-370 million years ago when the predominant
    rocks laid down were sandstones (Table 2).

Dip, dipping: inclined beds of rock which were deposited horizontally
    but tilted by later earth movements.

Drift: unconsolidated mixed material of sand and gravel deposited
    by ice or its meltwater: includes the term till (q.v.).

Dripstone: lime (calcium carbonate) precipitated underground from
    moving water in the form of stalactites,   stalagmites or pillars.

Drumlin: a low rounded hill formed of glacial drift and produced,
    often in numbers, beneath a moving ice-sheet.

Dyke: a narrow band of igneous rock injected into a vertical crack.

Esker: a steep-sided ridge of sand and gravel deposited within or
    underneath a melting ice-sheet by a river.

Eutrophication: a process of enrichment or fertilization of water
    which is most often caused artificially by pollution.   A eutrophic
    habitat is rich in minerals and productive of biomass.

Facies: a unit of rock representing a specific environmental
    condition, e.g., a delta.

Fault: a crack in rock along which movement has taken place.

Flush: mineral enrichment caused by moving water;   usually applied
    to an acid environment.

Foraminifera: minute floating plants with a perforated shell of
    calcium carbonate.

Glacial: of an ice age, usually the most recent one in the Pleistocene
    (q.v.):   also the phase of ice advance during such a time.

Glacial lake: a lake occurring during the melting of an ice sheet,
    often impounded by the ice itself.

Glacial relict: an organism which has persisted since the Pleistocene
    (q.v.) despite the warming of the climate.

Glacial spillway: the exit channel of a glacial lake which may
    cut through hills or ridges unrelated to the present drainage
    of an area.

Gneiss: a metamorphic banded rock somewhat like granite.

Goniatite: an extinct mollusc with a spiral compartmented
    shell.

Greywacke: a sandstone with sand fragments mixed with much
    finer sediments.

Hummock-hollow (pool): describes one method of bog growth where
    moss cushions alternate with shallow pools.

Hydrosere: the succession of plant types that occurs as a
    wet habitat becomes drier through the accumulation of sediment.

Igneous: a rock produced from molten material either above or
    below the ground.

Inlier: an area of older rocks surrounded by younger ones, for
    example in the heart of a rock fold.

Interglacial: a warm phase between two advances of ice (glacials).

Introduced: a plant or animal originally brought to Ireland by
    man but now surviving without his help.

Intrusive: an igneous rock injected beneath the surface of the
    ground.

Invertebrate: one of the great majority of animals without a
    backbone, e.g., an insect, crab or snail.

Karst: bare limestone country where rainwater has produced
    many features by solution, e.g., caves, pavement, turloughs.

Lichen: a lower plant without stem or leaves, usually greyish in
    colour, and growing on rocks or tree bark.

Littoral: of the seashore, taken to extend to the limit of attached
    seaweed.

Liverwort: a small trailing bryophyte, usually requiring more
    humid conditions than a moss.

Lusitanian: describes an organism whose centre of distribution
is in north-west Spain or Portugal.

Machair: flat areas of calcareous dune grassland, grazed by animals:
    a western community found on sand with a high shell content.

Marl: a white deposit of calcium carbonate in lakes, derived
    partly from the remains of plants, especially the stoneworts
    (charophytes).

Mesolithic: a human culture of hunters and fishers with small flint
    implements which existed in Ireland from about 8000-5000 years
    before the present.

Micrite: a pure form of limestone precipitated from water.

Namurian: part of the Upper Carboniferous period (Table 2) when shales and sandstones were laid down in this country.

Old Red Sandstone: sandstones derived from the desert sands of the Devonian (Table 2).

Oligotrophic: a habitat poor in the minerals required for plant growth, usually acidic in character.

Oolite: a limestone formed of small rounded nodules of lime.

Ordovician: the period 500-430 million years ago whose marine conditions in Ireland produced shales and sandstones (Table 2).

Palaeozoic: the time 600-225 million years ago when the dominant life forms were invertebrates and later fish and amphibians.

Passerine: the group of small birds which perch, e.g., thrushes, tits, finches.

Pavement: sheets of exposed rock with regular cracks giving square or diamond-shaped blocks.

Permo-Trias: a period 270-180 million years ago which saw the development of the reptiles (Table 2).

Pingo: a dome-shaped hill with an ice-core, formed in tundra areas.

Pleistocene: the Ice Age, extending from 2 million to 10,000 years before the present (Table 2). It represents the early part of the Quaternary period.

Podsol: a nutrient-poor acid soil in which minerals have been washed out of the upper layers and have accumulated lower down.

Pre-Cambrian: the most ancient period (Table 2).

Pyroclastic: rocks derived from fragments produced in volcanic eruptions.

Quaternary: the latest period of geological time including the Ice Age and subsequent time.

Raised beach: an old shoreline of the sea some way above the present one; formed when sea-level was higher or the land, lower.

Reef-knoll: a shelly mudbank in the Carboniferous sea, now seen as a fossiliferous lens of rock in the limestone.

Regeneration: the replacement of mature trees in a woodland by seedlings.

Sedimentary structure: features formed within rocks during their deposition, e.g., ripple marks, rain pits.

Seral: describes a transitory stage in some vegetational change.

Silurian: the period 430-400 million years ago (Table 2).

Sink-hole: a hollow or pot-hole in limestone caused by solution or collapse.

Skarn: a mineral assemblage produced by metamorphism of calcareous rocks.

Solifluction: the slippage of surface soils on a layer of frozen ground that occurs in tundra conditions close to an ice sheet.

Stratification: a layering of the water in a lake caused by density differences.

Stratigraphic: of the description and ageing of layers of rock.

Striae: scratches on rock caused by stones held in moving ice.

Syenite: an alkaline igneous rock intruded close to volcanic activity.

Till: the mixed material deposited by an ice-sheet or glacier.

Trilobite: an extinct marine animal rather like a large woodlouse. Their fossil remains occur widely in Lower Palaeozoic rocks.

Tuff: a rock formed of consolidated volcanic ash.

Turbidite: a sedimintary rock laid down by currents on a continental slope.

Turlough: a temporary shallow lake in limestone country which fills and empties through cracks in response to the local water table.

Type locality/section: the place or rock exposure from which an organism or rock type was first described and named.

Unconformity: a break in the regular laying down of sedimentary rocks either caused by a period of non-deposition or of erosion.

Understorey: the layer of shrubs and young trees that occurs beneath the canopy of a woodland.

Visean: the upper part of the Carboniferous limestones.

TABLE 2: <u>Scale of geological and later time</u> (Figures represent the beginning of periods)

ERA	PERIOD	EPOCH	Human Culture in Ireland only		YEARS AGO
CENOZOIC	Quaternary		Iron age		2000
			Bronze age		4000
			Neolithic		5500
			Mesolithic		8500
		Holocene			10000
		Pleistocene			2 million
	Tertiary				70 million
MESOZOIC	Cretaceous				135 million
	Jurassic				180 million
	Triassic				225 million
PALAEOZOIC	Permian				270 million
	Carboniferous				350 million
	Devonian				400 million
	Silurian				430 million
	Ordovician				500 million
	Cambrian				600 million
PRE-CAMBRIAN					4500 million

7. BIBLIOGRAPHY

AN FORAS FORBARTHA, 1969, _Protection of the National Heritage_, Dublin.

AN FORAS FORBARTHA, 1977, _Inventory of Outstanding Landscapes_, Dublin.

AN FORAS FORBARTHA, 1975, _A Preliminary Survey of Irish lakes_, Dublin.

AN FORAS FORBARTHA, 1980, _Peatland Sites of Scientific Interest in Ireland_, A Report for the Wildlife Advisory Council, Dublin.

BAYNES, E.S.A., 1973, _A Revised Catalogue of Irish Macrolepidoptera_ (Butterflies and Moths), Hampton.

CABOT, D. 1979, Wildlife: in Gillmor (ed): _Irish Resources and Land Use_, Dublin.

CHARLESWORTH, J.K. 1966, _The Geology of Ireland: An Introduction_ Edinburgh.

COUNCIL OF EUROPE, 1979, _Explanatory Report Concerning the Convention on the Conservation of European Wildlife and Natural Habitats_, Strasbourg.

CRAMP, S., BOURNE, W.R.P., and SAUNDERS, D. 1974, _The Seabirds of Britain and Ireland_, London.

FAIRLEY, J.S., 1975, _An Irish Beast Book_, Belfast.

FOREST and WILDLIFE SERVICE, 1974, Report on Wetlands of of International and National Importance in the Republic of Ireland, Department of Fisheries and Forestry, Dublin.

GOODWILLIE, R., 1980, _European Peatlands_, Council of Europe, Strasbourg.

HUTCHINSON, C., 1979, _Ireland's wetlands and their birds_, Dublin.

IUCN THREATENED PLANTS COMMITTEE, 1979, _List of Rare Threatened and Endemic Plants in Europe_, Council of Europe, Strasbourg.

MITCHELL, F. 1976, _The Irish Landscape_, London.

McCRACKEN, E. 1971, _The Irish Woods since Tudor Times_, Newton Abbott.

NATURE CONSERVANCY COUNCIL, 1980, _A Draft Community List of Threatened Species of Wild Flora and Vertebrate Fauna_, Vols I and II. A Report prepared for the Commission of the European Economic Community.

NEVILL, W.E., 1963, Geology and Ireland, Dublin.

NOIRFALISE, A. and VANESSE, R. 1976, Heathlands of Western Europe, Council of Europe, Strasbourg.

NI LAMHNA, E. (ed) 1979, Provisional distribution atlas of amphibians, reptiles and mammals in Ireland, An Foras Forbartha, Dublin.

O'GORMAN, F. (ed) 1980, The Irish Wildlife Book, Dublin.

ORME, A.R., 1970, The World's Landscapes-Ireland, London.

PARSLOW, J.F.L., and EVERETT, M.J., 1980, Threatened Birds in Europe, Council of Europe, Strasbourg.

PERRING, F. and WALTERS, S.M. (eds) 1976, Atlas of the British Flora, London.

PRAEGER, R.L. 1972, The Natural History of Ireland, Wakefield.

PRAEGER, R.L. 1974, The Botanist in Ireland, Wakefield.

RATCLIFFE, D.A. 1977, A Nature Conservation Review, Cambridge.

ROHAN, P.K., 1975, The Climate of Ireland, Dublin

RUTTLEDGE, R.F. 1975, A List of the Birds of Ireland, Dublin.

SHARROCK, J.T.R. (ed) 1976, The Atlas of Breeding Birds in Britain and Ireland, Tring.

STEPHENS, N. and GLASSCOCK, R.E. 1970, Irish Geographical Studies, Belfast.

TANSLEY, A.G., 1939 The British Islands and their Vegetation, Cambridge.

WEBB, D.A., 1977, An Irish Flora, Dundalk.

WENT, A.E.J., and KENNEDY, M. 1969, A List of Irish Fishes, Dublin.

WHITTOW, J.B., 1974, Geology and Scenery in Ireland, Harmondsworth.